Wandering Educators Press

The Definitive Guide to Moving to Southeast Asia: Cambodia

By Gabrielle Yetter

Table of Contents

Preface

The first in our series of guides on Moving to Southeast Asia, *The Definitive Guide to Moving to Southeast Asia: Cambodia* is at once a detailed guide to success in moving to Cambodia, and an ode to the joy of living there. Author Gabrielle Yetter is the perfect guide to Cambodia – an expat herself, she's already done all the things that you need to do to thrive in Cambodia. With this book, you hold an insider's guide to the best of Cambodia. It's packed with great tips, excellent resources, and hard-earned knowledge. Sit back, put your feet up, and get ready to be inspired. I have a feeling we'll see you in Cambodia! Be sure to visit our Facebook page to share your experiences in Cambodia, ask questions of the author, and stay updated with new things that are happening every day!

Dr. Jessie Voigts, Publisher, WanderingEducators.com

Introduction

My love affair with Southeast Asia started in 2007 when my husband, Skip, and I honeymooned in Thailand - and our two-week trip turned into a journey that would change our lives. We fell in love with the gentleness, warmth, and spirituality of the people and decided we wanted to experience more, launching us on a quest for opportunities to move to this part of the world. Eventually, we came across VIA (Volunteers In Asia), and a couple of months after applying, received notice of two posts working with NGOs in Cambodia.

So began the process of elimination and change. We sold our home in Massachusetts, got rid of our cars, found a home for our cat Gracie, and gave away most of our stuff. In June 2010, we found ourselves with a one-way ticket on a plane headed for Phnom Penh, not completely sure what we were doing but very excited at the prospect of starting a new chapter in our lives.

My world has always been somewhat nomadic. I was born in India to an English mother and Maltese father, grew up in Bahrain, worked as a journalist in South Africa, traveled constantly, worked at Club Med in Mexico and Turkey, and eventually landed in the U.S. where I published a dining guide, worked for a newswire organisation, ran my own small business, married Skip, and settled into a comfortable lifestyle in Massachusetts.

And while I've always loved the places I've lived, I've never found anything quite like Cambodia. It's a country that is gentle yet rough around the edges, spiritual yet tainted by corruption, beautiful yet dreadfully harsh in its poverty. But it's a place where everyone smiles. And it has captured my heart.

Geography & Culture

Cambodia is a square-shaped country of 14 million people, bordered by Vietnam in the southeast and east, Thailand in the west and northwest, and Laos in the northeast. The coastal regions in the south and west border the Gulf of Thailand, and the mighty Mekong River (the 12th longest river in the world) traverses the country from north to south.

There isn't much elevation in the country, as the highest mountain measures only 1,771 metres and is located in the eastern part of the Cardamom Mountains (running across the southwest of the country). These mountains are lush and covered with virgin rainforest, spanning a range of more than one million hectares - said to represent Southeast Asia's greatest natural resource. Within this mountain range are hundreds of birds, plants, and animal species, including elephants, pleated gibbons, and Siamese crocodiles, as well as excellent opportunities for hiking, trekking, and boating.

Farther north, the Siem Reap region is dominated by the enormous Tonle Sap, which is known as Cambodia's Great Lake - responsible for more than 70 percent of the country's protein since it is a major source of fish. Located 15km south of the town, this body of water measures 2,500 sq km in the dry season and swells to 12,000 sq. km in the rainy season, making it one of the largest freshwater lakes in Asia. The lake drains into the Tonle Sap River which meanders southeast, eventually merging with the Mekong at Phnom Penh.

One of the fascinations about this river is that during the wet season, a unique phenomenon occurs causing the river to reverse direction, filling the lake instead of draining it. This happens when the Mekong becomes bloated with snow melt from China and Tibet as well as runoff from the monsoon rains during the wet season, and backs up into the Tonle Sap River at the point where the rivers meet in Phnom Penh. This forces the waters of the Tonle Sap back upriver into the lake. If you're in Phnom Penh at this time (sometime in November), you'll actually observe a difference between one day and the next when the river has changed direction.

Wherever you travel throughout Cambodia, you'll always see one thing: rice fields. Approximately 80 percent of the country's population lives in rural areas, and 71 percent depend primarily on agriculture (largely rice) for their livelihood.

While most of the country consists of flat plains, there are wonderful sights to behold when travelling across it. You'll see workers planting rice in the paddies, buffaloes bathing in mud puddles, lush vegetation (during rainy season) in the mountains of the northeast, huge lakes for swimming, jungles for trekking, and islands for exploring.

Some of the more popular places to visit include:

Siem Reap. Home of the magnificent Angkor Wat temple complex – a jaw-dropping collection of ancient ruins, some of which date back to the 9th century. Siem Reap is the area most visited by tourists in Cambodia, so it's best to go during the off season (rainy season) or mid-week if you don't want it to be overrun with crowds. I also find it best to visit the temples in the midday heat of the day (when everyone runs for shade or goes for lunch) or late in the afternoon just before they close at 5 or 6pm (depending on the temple) if you want to share it with fewer people. In addition to the temples, the town of Siem Reap has a wonderful, lively energy, bursting with restaurants, bars, spas, and markets - and there's plenty to do for at least several days.

Hot tip: Visit the Silk Farm on the outskirts of town for a glimpse into the entire process of silk making, from worm to loom.

9

Kep. This little seaside town on the south coast is one of our favourite weekend getaways. Firstly, it's an easy 3 ½ hour bus ride from Phnom Penh. Secondly, there's not a lot to do so it's a great place to relax, lie in a hammock, or watch the sunset. It's not a place for nightlife, shopping, or tourist attractions, as it's a sleepy haven with some of the best crab you'll ever taste. There are a handful of places to stay - and it's also the kick-off point for the 30-minute boat trip to Rabbit Island.

Hot tip: Take a hike into the Kep National Park while it is still rugged and unspoiled (there are plans to build a road through it).

Rabbit Island. There are a number of islands off the Cambodian coast, but Rabbit Island is the easiest to get to. The half-hour boat ride from Kep ($7 if you share a boat) takes you to this tiny island, occupied only by a handful of beach huts (which you can rent for less than $10/night) and a few local restaurants on the sand.

Hot tip: Get a massage at one of the small wooden platforms set up on the beach, where $7 buys you an hour of pampering with the sound of the waves lapping next to you.

Kampot. Located 30 minutes from Kep, Kampot is situated on the Kampot River and is a delightful place to visit for a weekend. There are some lovely eco-lodges on the river (about 15 minutes out of town) as well as fascinating caves to explore, pagodas, and a local market. Kampot is known for producing one of the best peppers in the world and you can visit pepper plantations and taste the spice right off the vine. A new casino resort opened in 2012 at the top of Bokor Mountain if you're looking for glitz and nightlife.

Hot tip: Don't miss the incredible firefly boat trip ($2 for one hour) which leaves from Les Manguiers eco-lodge every evening.

Sihanoukville. Also located on the south coast, Sihanoukville has a reputation for being a little on the edgy side, which it is in some areas such as Victory Beach and Occheuteal Beach, where there are lots of bars and nightlife. Otres, Serendipity, and Independence Beach are more appealing for visitors wanting a more laid-back experience and there are day trips to waterfalls, national parks, and a handful of beautiful islands off the coast

Hot tip: Take an excursion to Lazy Beach on Koh Rong Sanloem where you can stay in cabins, swim in warm waters, dangle in a hammock and while away the days in perfect tranquility. Space is limited as there are only 17 bungalows on the island (making it extremely private) and reservations are essential, particularly in high season.

Koh Kong. Koh Kong is in the far west of the country on the border with Thailand (so it's a popular destination for visa runs). It's a wonderful place to visit if you enjoy the outdoors, as you can go hiking in the Cardamom Mountains, kayaking on the river, and scuba diving in the Gulf of Thailand.

Hot tip: Take a day tour of trekking in the jungle, where you'll feel as though you're the only people for miles around.

Other areas worth exploring to get a taste of Cambodia are Battambang (ride the bamboo train and see the bat cave), Kratie (cross the river to Koh Trong for the pomelos and homestays), Mondulkiri (visit the amazing Bou Sra waterfall), and Ratanakiri (see the crystal clear volcanic crater lake. It's a very long and bumpy bus ride to this part of the country, so make sure you have more than a couple of days there).

History

Cambodia is mostly known for its recent history of the 1970s, when the dictator Pol Pot seized power and inflicted genocide on the country, brutally killing almost two million of his own people. Everyone you meet in Cambodia has a story of losing relatives or friends to this mass execution, and the trials of the perpetrators are being conducted at the time of writing this book.

Cambodia gained independence in 1953 and became a constitutional monarchy, but this happened only after centuries of conflict, territorial struggle, and invasion by other nations.

Between the 9th and 15th centuries, Cambodia witnessed the rise and fall of the mighty Khmer Empire with Angkor as its center of power. During that period, widespread conversion to Theravada Buddhism took place. This is the religion that the majority of Cambodians practice today.

The period lasting from the 15th to the 19th century is known as the "dark ages," since it consisted of four centuries of decline and territorial loss. During the 16th century, the country enjoyed a brief period of prosperity, when Spanish and Portuguese adventurers and missionaries came to visit, and the Cambodian kings promoted trade with other parts of Asia. The country contained flourishing trading communities from China, Indonesia, Malaysia, Japan, Spain, and Portugal, later joined by England and Holland, and created a cosmopolitan environment for business. But in 1594, the Siamese conquest of the new capital of Longvek marked a downturn in the country's fortunes, and Cambodia became caught in the power struggles between Siam (present-day Thailand) and Vietnam. As a result of the fall of Longvek, Siam ruled Cambodia for most of the next 300 years.

Vietnam's settlement of the Mekong Delta led to its annexation of that area at the end of the 17th century, causing Cambodia to lose this rich territory and become cut off from the sea.

By the 19th century, Cambodia had become a helpless pawn in the power struggles between Siam and Vietnam. Fortunately, France intervened (in competition with Britain, which shut it out of most parts of Southeast Asia) and provided the country with a new lease on life.

It was during this time that the French naturalist Henri Mahout rediscovered the ruins at Angkor, thereby piquing the interest of the

French for this part of the world. In 1863, the French concluded a treaty with King Norodom, providing them with the rights to explore and exploit the country's mineral and forest resources. Cambodia continued as a protectorate of France from 1863 to 1953.

In 1955, Sihanouk abdicated in favour of his father in order to participate in politics, and was elected Prime Minister. Upon his father's death in 1960, Sihanouk again became head of state, and during the Vietnam War, adopted an official policy of neutrality in the Cold War (though considered to be sympathetic to the communist cause). He allowed the Vietnamese communists to use Cambodia as a sanctuary and supply route for their arms and aid to forces fighting in South Vietnam, but when visiting Beijing in 1970, was ousted by a military coup led by Prime Minister General Lon Nol.

North Vietnamese and Viet Cong forces launched armed attacks on the new government and civil war ensued.

As the Vietnamese communists gained control of Cambodian territory, they imposed a new political infrastructure, which was eventually dominated by the Cambodian communists known as the Khmer Rouge.

Between 1969 and 1973, the Republic of Vietnam and the U.S. bombed and briefly invaded Cambodia. The Khmer Rouge reached Phnom Penh in 1975 and took power under the leadership of Pol Pot, who changed the name of the country to Democratic Kampuchea, modelling itself on Maoist China.

During the next four years, Cambodia experienced a period of devastation. Cities were evacuated, people were brutally forced to work as slaves in the rice fields, and almost two million people were massacred. Education, religion, and culture were virtually wiped out and temples, libraries, and western-style structures were destroyed.

17

In 1979, the People's Republic of Kampuchea, supported by the
Vietnamese, liberated Phnom Penh. The refusal of Vietnam to
withdraw from Cambodia led to economic sanctions by the U.S. and
its allies, making reconstruction virtually impossible and leaving the
country deeply impoverished.

Throughout the 1980s, Cambodia rebuilt its economy with the
assistance of the Vietnamese, which withdrew in 1989 when peace
efforts began in Paris.

In 1991, a Paris Peace Accord created the United Nations
Transitional Authority in Cambodia (UNTAC) and was backed by
22,000 UN troops in preparing the first free and fair general election
that was held in 1993 under the leadership of King Norodom
Sihanouk.

This newly-won stability was shaken up in 1997 by a coup d'etat led by the co-Prime Minister Hun Sen against the non-communist parties in the government, and many non-communist politicians were murdered.

Since then, Cambodia has lived in relative peace. The second commune elections were held in April 2007, followed by National Assembly elections in July 2008 and, in both cases, there was little of the pre-election violence that preceded the 2002 and 2003 elections. Both polls resulted in victories for the Cambodian People's Party, with the Sam Rainsy Party emerging as the main opposition party, and the royalist parties showing weakening support.

There are, however, constant problems with land rights, human trafficking, political rights, sexual crimes, and human rights. Hun Sen has been Prime Minister since 1985, making him the longest serving leader in Southeast Asia.

Weather & Temperature

There are two seasons in Cambodia: One is hot; the other is rainy and hot.

The rainy season runs from May to October, which means it rains almost every day. Sometimes it's only for an hour or less and sometimes it can go on for several hours – but it's nothing like parts of the world where you get constant drizzle for days on end. Rain in Cambodia is impressive. It often begins with a gentle wind which quickly escalates into a strong gust, bending trees and plants and sending cyclists running for cover. You'll generally see torrents of water pouring from the sky, sometimes accompanied by claps of thunder and brilliant flashes of lightning in a fabulous display of nature. While it may be stimulating to watch, lightning in Cambodia is far from welcome for rural communities, as it's the cause of many deaths among farm workers (in 2012, 103 people died from lightning strikes).

Since Cambodia lies 10 – 13 degrees north of the equator, the climate is tropical and temperatures can get as high as 40 degrees Celsius (104 degrees Fahrenheit) in the hottest months, accompanied by high humidity, which leaves you dripping with sweat and in search of anywhere with good air-conditioning. The best time of the year is between November and February when it can fall as low as 18 – 20 degrees Celsius (64 – 68 degrees Fahrenheit) after the sun goes down, and locals are often seen during this season wearing down jackets, gloves, and scarves.

Religion

More than 90 percent of Cambodians are Buddhist. Everywhere you go, you'll see curling spires of pagodas and bell-shaped *stupas* (tombstones holding ashes of deceased Buddhists) and hear the early-morning chant of monks summoning worshippers to special ceremonies – for the dead, for the newlyweds, for their ancestors, and for a multitude of occasions which require a monk.

When Cambodian businesses open a new location, monks are always summoned to bless it. When a couple gets on in years, their children bring in the monks for an aging ceremony. When a baby is born, monks come to bless and name the infant. Not much of significance is done in Cambodia without consulting the monks first. They are even used to select an auspicious date for important ceremonies or christenings.

According to their religion, Theravada monks can only eat two meals daily and are not allowed to prepare food themselves, so the lay Buddhists in the community cook and serve the monks - which also earn them merit for their next lives.

Religion is a huge part of Cambodians' lives and it's apparent in the way they conduct themselves, since the acts they do in this life reflect on the next life they are preparing for. Many a time we have been surprised and taken aback when a tuktuk driver has returned money from a fare we overpaid, or a market owner has run after us with a bag we left behind in his shop. Once, we left behind a packet of items from a pharmacy in a food stall at the always-busy Russian Market and returned 24 hours later to have the owner of the stall run over to us, clutching our packet, happy to see we had returned for it.

Under the Khmer Rouge, religion was one of the casualties, since the oppressive regime forbid any practice - and particularly targeted Buddhism, Islam, and Christianity. In today's much freer society, there are a number of other religions represented in Cambodia in addition to Buddhism. There are a couple of small Muslim communities (primarily in towns and rural fishing villages on the banks of the Tonle Sap and Mekong rivers), a small but growing Christian community, as well as Jewish centres and an emerging Mormon community.

Almost every home and business displays a small shrine (spirit house) containing fresh fruit, incense, flowers, and other offerings of food. They are often positioned in an auspicious location (which has been determined by a monk). It's important that you take care not to disturb them, since they are regarded as shelter for departed loved ones and have special significance in the home (or business). Our local supermarket, for instance, has a spirit house in front of the customer service desk with a notice which reads "Please do not stand in front of the God house."

Cambodians are also a very superstitious race of people. They are fearful of ghosts, some believe that black cats carry the spirits of the dead, and most practice traditional healing methods of rubbing coins on the skin to rid the body of "bad air."

Languages

Before we came to Cambodia, we'd never heard of Khmer (the native language), never mind know how to pronounce it. It's not pronounced as it is written and the right way to say it is "Khmai" if you want to sound like a local. Despite months of language classes and a private tutor, I still have lots of challenges, as there are so many inflections to a word that it's easy to say it wrong. And heaven help you if you do, since Cambodians will look at you as though you've just told them there's a flock of birds about to land on their head, if you don't say it exactly right.

While English is fairly widely understood in the main tourist regions of Phnom Penh, Siem Reap, and parts of the coast, it is an alien sound when you get outside the cities. People in the provinces generally won't have a clue what you're saying, so the only thing to do is gesture wildly, point to items on menus, practice charades, and smile (or laugh, depending on the circumstances) until you figure it out.

Having said that, it's important to master a few words and phrases since Cambodians love it when foreigners speak to them in their native tongue and will *always* comment on your good use of their language (even if you only say one word). Some important phrases to know are *"ar-koon"* (thank you), *"sua s'day"* (hello), *"lee hi"* (good bye), *"som kot loy"* (the check please), and *"rik ree-yay dile baanskole neak"* (it's nice to meet you). You'll also often be saying *"ottay, ar-koon"* (no thank you) to all the tuktuk drivers and motodops who constantly offer you a ride, at all times of the day or night.

If you decide to take the plunge and study the language, it's best to get a private tutor, as there are dozens of teachers around town offering their services (check on the Cambodian Parents' Network Yahoo group – see *"What to do when you first arrive"*), or you can enrol in a class at one of the following schools (prices are generally $4 - $10 per hour):

Khmer School of Language
Tel: +855 (0)23 213047
Email: adk.kslcamb@online.com.kh
52G Street 454 (near Russian Market),
Phnom Penh
http://www.cambcomm.org.uk/ksl

Khmer Friends Language School
Tel: +855 (0) 17606056
20, Street 185,
Phnom Penh
http://khmerfriends.org

LINK (Language Institute of Natural Khmer)
Tel: +855 (0)12 293 764Sovannaphumi School, 4th Floor
Street 200, between Norodom Blvd and Street Pasteur (51)
Phnom Penh
http://www.naturalkhmer.com

Disability Access

Cambodia is a challenging place for people with disabilities. There are no codes for equipping buildings for handicapped access and even the simplest task - such as getting across town - can be a major challenge. Getting into a tuktuk requires a big step up (or down), most buildings don't have elevators (we climb 47 steps to our apartment), and there are no revolving doors or ramps in public buildings. Even the sidewalks possess a challenge - even for those of us without physical disabilities - as they are generally rough, potholed, and littered with garbage in many areas of most cities.

The only way a person with physical disabilities would be able to travel comfortably in Cambodia would be to stay in a decent hotel, travel by taxi, and dine in ground floor restaurants.

Safety

Since moving to Cambodia almost two years ago, I've never felt threatened, unsafe, or endangered in any way. I walk everywhere, explore neighbourhoods, and travel around the country on buses and motorbikes. Having said that, however, it's a place where you do need to exercise caution as the cities (Phnom Penh and Siem Reap, in particular) possess an edginess that can turn unpleasant if you don't handle yourself correctly.

These are some of the things I'd suggest *not* doing: drinking a dozen beers and trying to find your way home at 3am; walking alone as a woman late at night; expressing anger or showing aggression to a Cambodian native (everything, even confrontations, are handled with smiles); getting into a traffic accident or physical incident and sticking around (we've heard of foreigners who are blamed, no matter what, when in confrontation with a local); using an ATM at night; carrying a bag over your shoulder; carrying anything valuable; riding on the back of a motodop (motorcycle taxi).

A few months after moving here, I had my bag snatched from my shoulder by a moto driver on the street where I live one night while walking home from dinner with my husband. It wasn't late and I wasn't alone or walking in an unknown area – but I subsequently discovered this was part of Phnom Penh living, and that I had now been unofficially initiated into Cambodian life.

I then heard about moto drivers who work in pairs, where the driver of the first bike snatches a bag from a pedestrian and the second one watches out to make sure they get away safely and tackles anyone who puts up resistance. Almost everyone I know here has experienced petty theft in some way (mostly bag snatching or bicycle theft), and we've been told to leave nothing of value near a window as there are thieves who grab things through windows (even when there are bars on them or if you live on the third floor).

As with any country where poverty is rife, there's quite a bit of petty theft. After my bag was stolen, I started wearing a bum bag containing only the essentials for my evenings out and if I have to carry larger sums of money, I now tuck it into a pocket instead of carrying it in a purse. I'd also caution expats about riding on the back of a motorbike with a motodop. Not only are they not safe (there's a very high accident rate), but they also provide targets for thieves who might grab your bag from around your shoulder.

If you do fall victim to bag snatching, don't hold on. The contents of any bag can be replaced. Your body and your health can't.

If you experience a crime, you'll have to contact the Tourist Police (097 778 0002) in order to obtain a police report if you want to claim it on your insurance. You'll probably be asked to pay a bribe to the police officer in order to get the report (somewhere in the region of $5 - $10).

I have a friend who caught the woman who snatched her bag and ended up spending hours in the police station, followed by a trip to the jail, followed by a trip to the court. She ended up getting her bag back with most of the contents but had to pay a "fee" to the police as well as spend a lot of her time dealing with it.

Here's a list of emergency numbers that may be useful.

Police: 117 (from landlines), T: (023) 366 841; (023) 720 235 (from mobiles)

Fire: 118 (from landlines), T: (023) 723 555 (from mobiles)

Ambulance: 119 (from landlines) T: (023) 724 891 (from mobiles)

Tourist police: (012) 942 484 or (097) 778 0002

Full list: http://www.phnompenh.gov.kh/phnom-penh-city-emergency-useful-numbers-24-hrs-169.html

(NOTE: The international telephone dialing code for Cambodia is 855. When calling from overseas, drop the zero before the phone number. When dialing within the country, dial zero and the eight digits which follow).

Other than petty theft, there's another hazard to being a pedestrian in Cambodia – traffic. It's mostly a source of amusement, as I've never seen anything quite like it – tuktuks drive the wrong way on one-way roads, motos carry everything from pigs to six-foot plates of glass to their entire families (the most I've seen is six), and luxury SUVs believe they own the road. While traffic moves at a slow and meandering pace, it's a little overwhelming when you want to cross the road.

Rule of thumb is that motorbikes and tuktuks will generally go around you, but cars will not. Lexus SUVs, emblazoned with an eight-inch "LEXUS" on the door, seem intent on running down anything in their way – and generally smile as they do so – so it's wise to give them a wide berth. Vehicles will often not stop at stop signs or red lights. Traffic cops with whistles ineffectually try to direct cars and motorbikes, and everyone drives on the wrong side of the street if their destination is in sight.

There are also a number of SUVs and luxury cars with a "VIP" sticker displayed on the front dashboard. That could mean they are Cambodian bigwigs and you don't want to tangle with, get into an accident with, or have an argument with them. Their importance in Cambodian society will overshadow any sense of right or wrong, so keep your peace with them.

Visas

Cambodia is one of the easiest countries in the world to get into. Visas are inexpensive and simple and there are no requirements for having one.

Before arriving, you can get your visa online in three days by going to the Ministry of Foreign Affairs website: http://www.mfaic.gov.kh/evisa/, instead of going to a Cambodian embassy or getting it when you land. Fill out the online application form and pay with your credit card. Once the visa is emailed to you, print two copies and bring them with you. Make sure your passport does not expire within six months of your arrival.

You can also get a visa "on arrival" at Phnom Penh and Siem Reap airports as well as at the six international border crossings with

Thailand, some of Vietnam's international border crossings, and at the main border crossing with Laos.

When you arrive, go to the Visa On Arrival desk, where your application will be reviewed and you will receive a visa within minutes. It's one of the simplest and easiest processes I've found anywhere.

The only problem with the e-Visa, however, is that it only operates as a tourist visa, so business travellers who need to stay longer or need a multiple entry visa will have to apply for a Cambodian business visa through the conventional channels at the airport on arrival.

A Cambodian tourist visa costs $20 for a 30 day visit ($5 more if you do it online) and does not allow for multiple entries. You can extend it for a further 30 days through a travel agency or the Immigration Department (on the road to the airport) at a cost of $15. Overstaying your visa will cost you a hefty $5 per day.

When your visa is getting close to expiration, it's time for a "visa run"— which is also a good excuse for a holiday to another country. All you need do is cross a border (even a bus trip to Vietnam or Thailand is fine), then turn around and come back into Cambodia so you can get another visa. There are a number of scams where border officials, drivers, and "guides" will insist you need their help or need to pay a fee. If you brush them off politely or ask for a receipt, they will probably move on to their next potential victim. It's advisable to take a passport sized photo with you, but you'll only be fined a dollar if you don't have one and need to get it at the border.

If you're staying longer than 30 days, it's advisable to request a business visa, which costs $25 and can be renewed indefinitely in increments of one month, six months, or one year at a time (be aware that the one and three month extensions are only single entry, whereas the six and 12 month options allow multiple entries and exits).

No questions are generally asked at customs for the short term work visa, and there's no need to provide any proof of employment.

A one-year work visa costs $290 and is usually provided by your employer.

Money & Banking

When we arrived in Cambodia, we were surprised to discover that, while the national currency is the riel, almost every transaction is conducted in U.S. dollars. The value of the dollar translates into approximately 4,000 riel and there are no coins, so your wallet will be lighter in weight, but you'll probably carry around lots of paper currency. The smallest note is the 100 riel, which translates into approximately 2.5 cents and we use it mostly for beggars and tipping.

Make sure to always carry a wad of single dollar bills since you'll need them constantly. It always amazes me that tuktuk drivers never have change so you'll need to have single dollars to pay them. Many small shops or *hang bais* (small restaurants or roadside stands) can't break large bills, and you'll often get change in riel if you're shopping in a local market.

Until 2006, there were no ATMs in Cambodia. However, there are now banks and ATMs everywhere, except for some of the smaller towns and rural areas. The large banks include ANZ, Acleda, Canadia, ABA, FTB (Foreign Trade Bank), and SBC, all of which dispense cash in dollars.

To open a bank account, all you need is your passport (containing your Cambodian visa) along with a letter from your employer (verifying you work here) or from your landlord (showing that you live here), and you'll have a bank account within hours. We found the process simple, pleasant, and pain free and were provided with an ATM card (with a profile photo on the back) as well as internet banking services. Banks are generally open 8am to 3pm or 4pm on Monday to Friday and some are open Saturday mornings.

One huge difference we've found between living here and in the western world is that Cambodia functions primarily as a cash country. Credit cards are generally not accepted at any businesses outside of Phnom Penh, Siem Reap, and Sihanoukville, and most transactions are done in cash. We pay our landlord in cash, pay for our internet services by dropping into their location once a month to pay (in cash), and never see a bill for anything.

You can also set up online payments for bills such as electricity, water, and internet with FTB and ABA if you don't want to deal with cash.

Take care not to accept torn bills when receiving change, though. Due to the commonness of forged currency in this country, many vendors and banks won't accept even slightly torn US dollar bills. We've had a torn bill returned to us by a street kid who we tipped for showing us around a temple, and our landlady scrutinises every bill in the rent money with the intensity of a homeless woman searching for a gold coin in a rubbish dump.

Taxes

Income tax is taken out of your salary by your employer and everyone's salary is taxed at the following rate:

Monthly Salary : From	To	Rate
0	$125.00	0%
$125.25	$312.50	5%
$312.55	$2,125.00	10%
$2,125.25	$3,125.00	15%
$3,125.25	upwards	20%

Fringe benefits such as housing and cars are also taxed and there are no other income taxes at this stage. Business owners pay profit taxes of 20 percent. Taxes are paid in riel – the General Department of Taxation provides a conversion rate in the event that salaries are paid in US dollars.

Vaccinations

Before travelling to Cambodia, we were advised by international clinics and multiple websites to get every inoculation under the sun. Much of the advice was precautionary and tended to err on the side of caution or fear, so we opted not to get them all but to protect ourselves from those diseases which were most prevalent and would make the biggest difference in our lives.

The ones we chose were hepatitis, typhoid, rabies, and Japanese encephalitis. We opted not to get malaria meds and have never heard of anyone getting the disease, even when travelling to outermost provinces, but it may be worth bringing along a supply if you think you'll be spending time in rural areas, particularly during rainy season.

Make sure you are up-to-date with routine shots, such as the measles/mumps/rubella (MMR) vaccine, diphtheria/pertussis/tetanus (DPT) vaccine, and poliovirus vaccine. You may want to seek advice from a specialist travel doctor - ideally one attached to a clinic that specialises in tropical medicine. Since having our shots, my doctor in Phnom Penh told me there's no longer a need to renew rabies inoculations since they are now only advising it for people who work closely with animals (such as vets or farmers) or travellers involved in any activities that might bring them into direct contact with bats, carnivores, and other mammals.

If, like us, you run out of time to get all your shots, you can complete them when you're in Phnom Penh at the International SOS Clinic or Tropical and Travellers Medical Clinic in Phnom Penh. You can also learn more from the Center for Disease Control and Prevention website.

One of the more common diseases in this region is dengue fever, which, unfortunately, has no preventative vaccine. It demonstrates many of the same symptoms as malaria and can easily be diagnosed by any good clinic in Cambodia. It is very unpleasant and may provide several weeks of discomfort and exhaustion and all that can be prescribed is bed rest, Paracetamol, plenty of liquids and regular blood monitoring.

And, of course, there's a pretty good chance of getting a gastric bug from contaminated food or water since hygiene is not up to western standards. When that happens, the local clinic will diagnose it, treat it, and prescribe the appropriate medications.

Bringing Your Pet

If you're bringing Fido or Fluffy along with you, you need to make sure their vaccinations are up to date and get a health certificate from your vet within 15 days of leaving your home country. You may or may not be asked for it at customs. If not, don't worry about it. Nobody else does.

A number of expats bring their pets to live in Cambodia and, while they stand out among dozens of filthy shaggy mutts who roam the streets, they seem to fare just fine. It's best to keep Fido on a leash and Fluffy inside as neighbourhood pets aren't usually cared for in the same way as western ones. The best vet in town is Agrovet, and all supermarkets stock food supplies that will keep them happy.

Transportation & Driving

One of the things we love most about living in Cambodia is not having a car. Gone are car insurance payments, hefty gas charges, and traffic frustration. When we want to get around, we walk or take a tuktuk (which costs $2 to get most places around town, $3 to travel long distances across the city and $7 to the airport).

While we love travelling this way as it brings us closer to street life and interaction with locals, there are sometimes a couple of hiccups along the way. For instance, every tuktuk driver will nod vigorously and enthusiastically say "Yes" when you ask if he knows how to find your destination. For a Cambodian, it's very important to never lose face - and admitting he doesn't know the way is like saying he doesn't want your business. So he'll head off happily... sometimes in the wrong direction. Once he realizes he's lost, he'll pull over and have a powwow with other drivers on the street who will assemble around a map and eventually get you on your way.

When we want to explore outside the perimeter of the tuktuk (such as when we're in coastal towns or visiting the villages), we rent motor bikes, as they open up a new world which is not suitable for four wheeled vehicles. There are rental outlets all over Phnom Penh and other cities, and most hotels and guesthouses will be able to line up a bike for you (usually costing between $5 and $10 per day).

Make sure you never ride without a helmet as motor accidents happen quite a bit since most drivers aren't particularly conscientious about looking both ways (or either way, in many cases). Good helmets can't be found in the countless shops all over town so invest in a good one or bring one with you if you'll be riding on a bike. There's a new KTM shop opposite Wat Langka which is a good place to start.

A law passed in July 2012 requires passengers and drivers to wear helmets. Sadly, like many things in Cambodia, it is rarely observed.

For longer distances we take buses, which are generally comfortable with air-conditioning, pit stops, and dubiously entertaining back-to-back Cambodian music videos lasting for hours. Buses to Siem Reap cost between $5 and $12 for a five to seven hour journey (the more expensive bus gets you there faster), trips to Kampot cost around $6 for a four hour ride (30 minutes less for Kep), and journeys to Koh Kong cost $6 - $8 for a six to seven hour trip. While buses are mostly reliable and comfy, it's important to remember you're in Cambodia and that things don't always go according to plan. They often run late, sometimes break down, and always make multiple stops to pick up locals along the road if they have empty seats to fill.

But that's also part of the adventure of living in a foreign country. I once found myself sitting next to a woman carrying a small tree, and another time rode for three hours on a plastic stool in the aisle of a bus travelling to Kampot because I boarded halfway through the trip when all the seats were filled.

If you don't care to travel by bus, there's the option of hiring a private taxi, which is cheap by western standards and faster than the bus. A taxi to Kep costs around $40 and one to Siem Reap will run around $70. The best way to find one is to ask your tuktuk driver (or a hotel, if you don't have a local driver), as he usually has a friend who drives a cab. You can also rent a private car, either with or without driver, when you want to go to areas that aren't on the regular bus or taxi routes.

Make sure you *never* get into a shared taxi unless you really want to experience Cambodia as a Cambodian. They are small minivans that pack in enough people to make a sardine can look spacious and are known to be treacherous on the roads. I was once on a business trip where a colleague and I were forced to take one, so I bought two seats for each of us so we could have enough space to breathe. It's been said that shared taxis sometimes even sell the seat *under* the driver!

If you decide you want to own a car in Cambodia, there are a number of auto dealers on Streets 108 and 106 in Phnom Penh (between

Norodom and Monivong) where you'll be able to negotiate for a vehicle if you take someone who speaks Khmer. Better still, check the Cambodian Parents' Network Yahoo group (see *"What to do when you first arrive"*) for vehicles being sold by expats who are leaving the country. There's also a casual car lot on the street near the Night Market where people park cars they want to sell with the phone number in the window.

For insurance coverage, check out Infinity and Forte which offer a variety of policies – third party starts around $90 and comprehensive is $300 plus. Insurance is important here, as you will be asked to pay compensation even if a moto hits **you** (plus various corrupt police fees which will probably go along with it).

In order to drive in Cambodia, you need a Cambodian driver's license. You can get one at a driving school or at Lucky Lucky Motor Cycle Shop on Monivong in Phnom Penh for a fee of approximately $40. All you need is a copy of your passport cover page and the page containing your visa, a copy of your current overseas license, and a couple of photos. No driving test is needed. If you don't own a valid foreign license, you can pay a fee of $140 to achieve the same result. Watch out for some of the driving school scams where they will try to charge you a lot more.

Make sure to have any prospective purchase inspected by a competent mechanic, since Cambodian roads are very rough on suspensions and it's not uncommon for a newly-purchased car to need repairs before you get it back on the road again. There are also cases of damaged American cars being imported, fixed up, and resold, so it's important to have expert assistance when you buy a car if you're not an expert yourself.

If you want a full time driver, expect to pay about $150 - $200 per month for their services (you provide the car).

And remember that, as with many things in Cambodia, some of the traffic rules don't make a lot of sense but need to be observed if you don't want a ticket. For example, it's illegal to drive with your lights on during the day, but legal to drive without them at night.

Electricity

The electrical current in Cambodia is 220 volts with electrical sockets taking two flat prongs, so you'll need a voltage converter unless your appliance or computer is dual voltage or designed for 220 volts.

However, most sockets are multi-plug that accept twin parallel and twin round 4mm (CEE 7/16 Europlug). These sockets will also accept twin round 4.8mm plugs (CEE 7/17 - German/French) which are the most reliable connection, but using these may destroy the socket for other pin types.

Adapters are cheap and widely available can be used for most plugs. We bought a universal adapter at the local market for 35 cents.

The power supply can be erratic at times, depending on location. My office near the Russian Market experiences regular outages, for example, so it's important to invest in a good surge protector (available all over the place at a fraction of the price you'd pay anywhere else in the world), since power rises and falls – and quits – with some frequency. There are also frequent outages in the rainy season and electricity is inconsistent in the rural areas.

The cost of electricity can run anywhere between $25 and $150 per month, depending on your use of air conditioning, other electrical appliances, and the size of your apartment.

Internet Accessibility

You'll get a wifi connection almost everywhere you go in Cambodia, whether you're staying in a $5/night guesthouse, sipping a latte in a Siem Reap coffee shop, or sitting in the airport waiting for your flight to Bangkok. It won't always be a good connection (and sometimes may be down for hours or days at a time), but most places advertise the fact that they have wifi. Many guesthouses or hotels and some of the coffee shops, such as Brown's and Spinelli's in Phnom Penh, even provide free computers which you use while you're on the road.

We've heard a number of stories from friends who've found their home internet access to be spotty or non-existent, but we've usually had good luck with ours – and have only lost the connection a handful of times (once when I forgot to pay the bill). There are many different internet providers, including Digi, Ezecom, Online Wifi

Max, Metfone, Beeline, and Hello, all of which offer different packages. Home internet service starts around $12/month and increases according to your package. We pay $24/month and it provides us with decent speed and rare outages. Sometimes there are a few problems with Skype and downloading videos (which take considerable time to stream), but otherwise we're happy campers.

For travel, you can get a dongle (a small device that looks like a USB flash drive and connects you to the internet) for approximately $40. It works anywhere in the country, speeds are around 700kb/s and you can buy scratch cards anywhere to add credit as you need it.

Attractions

Before moving to Cambodia, I lived in London, New York, and San Francisco - and often felt overwhelmed by the number of attractions, shows, events, festivals, and activities to do every day of the week.

Cambodia, for me, is much easier. While there may be a shortage of cultural attractions, it suits me fine to have a choice of 10 – 15 things to choose from each week, instead of selecting from 100 or more.

First, there are the obvious ones, which most people do within their first few weeks. The harrowing, yet fascinating, tours of the Killing Field and Tuol Sleng Genocide Museum are usually on the list of things to do, not only for the tourist aspect, but more importantly, for an insight into the psyche of these incredible people, many of whom have been to hell and back in their lifetimes.

The other sights on the tourist route are the Royal Palace and National Museum in Phnom Penh, Angkor Wat and the magnificent temples in Siem Reap, along with a number of other pagodas and shrines dotted throughout the country and the beaches and islands of the southern coast.

Living in Phnom Penh, there are many local things to do once you've run through those in your tour guide. There are dozens of activities organised by expats – from Hash House Harrier runs to cycling clubs, motor biking activities, bridge, salsa dancing, book clubs, amateur dramatics, netball and football matches, and yoga retreats.

There are several venues for live music and dancing as well as cultural centres, performance halls, theatres, and art galleries.

There's also a cozy little selection of movie theatres to choose from.

In Phnom Penh, The Flicks are small movie houses where you lounge on padded futons or wicker chairs and watch new films, documentaries, or foreign films in the air-conditioned spaces. Legend Cinema is the newest movie theatre in Phnom Penh, screening Hollywood hits. Platinum Cineplex in the Sorya Mall shows a combination of Khmer and English language films.

Meta House is a rooftop space run by the German Cambodian Cultural Centre where, almost every night, you can view a Cambodian documentary, foreign film, or art exhibit for only $2. The French Cultural Centre has frequent film screenings in French and Bophana screens a variety of documentary movies.

In Siem Reap, the only place to view movies belongs to the Siem Reap Film Society located above the ABOUTAsia office in Charming City (to the north of town). There's also a small cinema at the night market showing documentaries every night. In Sihanoukville, the Top Cat Cinema and Galaxy Cinema allow you to select a movie and rent the entire place for a small fee.

Outside the cities, there are dozens of places to go and things to do, from the beaches of Kep and Sihanoukville with their countless islands, to the caves of Kampot, the jungles of Koh Kong, mountains of Mondulkiri, and the river in Kratie.

And if there's not enough culture or excitement in Cambodia, you can hop on a 60-minute flight to Bangkok, where you'll be overwhelmed by choices that are not available here.

When you want to get a taste of the countryside and a different view of the city, or if you want to try a biking, hiking, boating or fishing adventure, the following companies provide some excellent options.

About Asia - Day tours in and around Siem Reap, Koh Kong, Takeo, Cambodia coast and more.   http://www.aboutasiatravel.com

Adventure Cambodia - Cycling, fishing, kayaking, local sights. http://www.adventure-cambodia.com

Adventure Loop - Touring, trekking, cycling and dirt bike tours. http://www.adventureloop.com

Angkor Explorer - Day tours of Siem Reap and Phnom Penh. http://www.angkorexplorer.com

Angkor Focus - Day tours in and around Siem Reap. http://www.angkorfocus.com

Asia Adventures - River trips, day tours, scuba, biking, trekking, fishing. http://www.asia-adventures.com

Betelnut Jeep Tours - Daytrips to the Phnom Tamao Wildlife Rescue Center. http://www.betelnuttours.com

Beyond Unique Escapes - Daytrips and cooking classes in and around Siem Reap (new tours planned for Battambang and Phnom Penh). http://www.beyonduniqueescapes.com

Buffalo Tours - Day tours in and around Siem Reap and Phnom Penh. http://www.buffalotours.com

Cambodia Boutique Travel - Cultural, historical, and food excursions around Phnom Penh. http://www.cambodiaboutiquetravel.com

Cambodia Cycling - off road and back road tours of the countryside and villages. http://www.cambodiacycling.com

Cambodia Uncovered - Day trips and boat trips around Phnom Penh and into Takeo, Kandal, Kampong Cham, Prey Veng, and Kampong Speu. http://www.cambodiauncovered.com

Capitol Tours - Day tours in various locations around Cambodia. http://www.capitoltourscambodia.com

Dancing Roads - Off road dirt bike tours, cycling and 4x4 tours. http://www.dancingroads.com

Derleng Tours - Day trips in Siem Reap and Phnom Penh. http://www.live.derlengtours.com

Exotissimo - Day tours in and around Siem Reap and Phnom Penh. http://www.exotissimo.com

Grasshopper Tours - Bicycle tours: (Phnom Penh, Siem Reap and Battambang). http://grasshopperadventures.com

Green Orange Kayak - Kayak tours in Battambang area - http://www.fedacambodia.org/fileadmin/images/Green_Orange_Kaya k.pdf

Hanuman Travel - Behind the scenes day tours to Phnom Tamao Wildlife Center, Phnom Chisor, Oudong, and other areas around Phnom Penh and Siem Reap. http://www.hanuman.travel

Helistar - Helicopter tours over Siem Reap (private tours elsewhere can be arranged). http://helistarcambodia.com

Hidden Cambodia - Dirt bike, 4WD, trekking, cycling, humanitarian tours, temples. http://www.hiddencambodia.com

Mango Cambodia - Daytrips to explore the city, countryside and history of Cambodia with an emphasis on off-the-beaten track excursions. http://mangocambodia.com

Phnom Penh Fishing tours - Weekend fishing trips in the Tonle Sap. Future plans include frog hunts, spider hunts, crab hunts, and cockroach hunts (for bait). Contact 0978970007.

www.fishinginphnompenh.wordpress.com

Phnom Penh Urban Adventures - Day tours in and around Phnom Penh. http://www.phnompenhurbanadventures.com

Khmer Architecture Tours - Tours focusing on Cambodian architecture and historical context of Phnom Penh, in cyclos, tuktuks, or vans. http://www.ka-tours.org

Unique Kayak Cambodia - Kayak tours in Siem Reap area. http://www.uniquekayakcambodia.com

Urban Adventures - Tours in and around Phnom Penh and Siem Reap. http://www.urbanadventures.com/search?cn=Cambodia

Free Things To Do

It doesn't cost much to do things in Cambodia. A tenner will buy you a night out with a meal and a movie - and many local dining spots serve main courses for the same cost as a grande latte in many parts of the world.

Even better, though, are things to do that cost nothing, and are just as much fun.

Phnom Penh's riverside is a hub of activity and a great place to take a walk or partake in the exercise classes which are held every night in the open. It works like this: Someone sets up shop with a boom box and a pair of sneakers, starts to jive or hip-hop, and dozens of people follow along. It costs nothing to join the action, though you should drop a donation in the box, and is a great way to get exercise (or embarrass yourself in public).

Many of the nightclubs in Phnom Penh provide free live music. Check out Equinox, Memphis, The Village, The Groove, Slur Bar, Latin Quarter, Sharky's, Paddy Rice, The Boathouse, and the FCC. Music listings are found online at LengPleng.com, and LadyPenh.com provides detailed listings of events around the city.

If you're looking for spiritual nourishment, there are meditation sessions at Wat Langka (Street 51 and Sihanouk Blvd) every Monday, Thursday, and Saturday from 6-7pm and on Sunday at 8.30am.

There are also lots of clubs around town run by expats (see "Attractions") and a handful of swimming pools which are free to use (often with the purchase of a drink or bite to eat).

But the best free thing to do is to explore. Walk the streets. Wander through local markets. Meander along the river. Talk to the locals. Smile at everyone.

What To Do When You First Arrive

The first thing to do when moving to Cambodia (or even before you arrive), is to join the Cambodian Parents' Network Yahoo group, which you can find online at:

http://groups.yahoo.com/group/cambodiaparentnetwork. You don't have to be a parent, as it's a Cambodian-based expat community online with more than 3,000 members and will be your biggest help in learning about anything and everything going on around town: places to rent, where to buy things, questions on health issues, updates on holiday spots, jobs or internships, and much more. It's the only place where you'll see people asking for pony-shaped cake moulds and honey baked hams, as well as advice on what to do if you get into a car accident or need healthcare for your cat.

During the time I've lived in Phnom Penh, through postings on CPN, I've joined a newly-formed book club as well as a film group. I've taken an Apsara dance class and bought a used computer as well as posted my own queries about places to get a couch cleaned and what's going on around town for Christmas. It's like having your own personal guide who will answer any question about Cambodia, as well as introduce you to people you might want to meet.

Once you land at the Phnom Penh International Airport, the best way to get into town is by tuktuk to get a feel of the real Cambodia (taxis are also available if you need them). I would suggest booking a hotel or guesthouse prior to arrival so you have a place to go. Most tuktuk drivers will understand you if you tell them the name of your location in English. It's also a good idea to have the street address (or map) written on a piece of paper that you can show them, in case they are not familiar with your destination.

There are dozens of hotels, hostels, and guesthouses around town and I'd suggest staying somewhere between Streets 178 and 400, east of Monivong Blvd. There are plenty of cheap guesthouses if you're not picky about the neighbourhood and I've never seen anything *really* bad. We stayed in a very basic $10/night guesthouse west of Monivong for the first three weeks and it was perfectly fine (and had air-conditioning) but you may keep in mind that Monivong bisects the city so that the cheap (local) neighbourhoods are on the west side with the more comfortable areas on the east.

A couple of areas you may want to avoid are where the girly bars proliferate, since they tend to be noisier and a bit seedier than other areas – Streets 104 and 136 are better known for these bars. While the riverside is a lovely spot to wander and people-watch, it also tends to be a little noisier at night if you're an early-bird or more interested in tranquil accommodation.

Another thing to do when you arrive is purchase a mobile phone. There are lots of shops around town where you can buy one for less than $20 (some are second-hand so you may want to find a reputable phone shop if you want a new one). You'll need to bring your passport and can purchase a SIM card for $10 - $30, depending on the phone number you want, then purchase a scratch card which will provide you with any amount of calling credit that you choose.

Housing

Some of the most frustrating and entertaining days of our first weeks in Phnom Penh were spent hunting for a place to live. Since standards are different from those we're used to in the western hemisphere, we saw a bit of everything. There were apartments with views of barbed wire fences, staircases with more than 80 steps winding through outside balconies (great for the rainy season), an apartment with no dining room, and one with separate entrances into each room from a central corridor. After working with a leasing agent for a few days, we ended up in a beautiful, spacious apartment with a huge wraparound balcony overlooking a leafy, tree-lined street close to the Independence Monument and within walking distance of everything.

Leasing agents are usually a great resource, as they know what's on the market and can negotiate for you in Khmer. In Cambodia, the landlords pay the fees, so an agent may not be as passionate as you are to drive the price down. There are, however, a number of other options well worth exploring before going down that route.

One of the best resources in the country is the Cambodian Parents' Network (see "*What to do when you first arrive*") – as you'll receive emails from people in the group who post notices about places to rent or sublet, mostly in Phnom Penh.

There are a number of websites which post notices about homes and apartments to rent (foreigners can only buy apartments if they are above the first floor). They include Expat Advisory, Khmer440, Cambodia rental classifieds, Bongthom, and the Phnom Penh Post classifieds.

- http://www.expat-advisory.com/
- http://www.khmer440.com/k/
- http://rentals.classifieds1000.com/Cambodia
- http://www.bongthom.com/
- www.phnompenhpost.com

It's also a good idea to walk or bike around the neighbourhoods to get an idea of where you want to live and look out for "For Rent" signs. BKK1 is the area where most expats live and it tends to be a little higher-priced that other neighbourhoods. We chose to live slightly outside BKK1, as it gives us more of a local flavour, yet still provides access to everything we need.

When you're exploring Phnom Penh, keep in mind that odd numbered streets run north to south, with the numbers increasing as you head west from the river. Even numbers run west to east and increase as you head south (with some exceptions). House numbers, however, are quite haphazard and there's no rhyme or reason to the numbering. Don't expect buildings to be numbered sequentially - and it's not uncommon to find two completely unrelated houses on the same street with the same number.

Apartments in Cambodia often lack some of the luxuries of home and it's pretty rare to find such conveniences as bathtubs and ovens. Most bathrooms have a shower head in the middle of the room (making the entire bathroom into the shower), and many kitchens have small or unsophisticated cooking equipment, unless you're renting in the higher bracket.

As with most things in this country, it's customary to negotiate on your housing. Our downstairs neighbours managed to get a new bathroom, have a wall knocked down in their dining room, and a total paint job done on their place when they decided to renew for three more years. It's helpful to have someone who speaks the language who can walk you through the process.

The cost of a decent apartment ranges from $250 to $800 per month, depending on the neighbourhood and the facilities. Serviced apartments are more expensive (generally starting around

$1,000/month) and usually include maid service, security, wifi, fitness rooms, and gyms. There are a number of them scattered around the city and several, such as Bassac Garden City and Jardins du Bassac, are enclosed compounds with security gates, swimming pools, tennis courts, squash courts, children's playgrounds, and fitness centres.

Apartments near the Russian Market, Tuol Sleng, and other places slightly out of the city centre tend to be cheaper and most places usually come sparingly furnished (we had to purchase extra pieces to fill out the space since our landlords had a specific budget in mind). Electricity is not usually included in the rent and foreigners are charged a higher rate than Khmers – usually between $25 and $150/month, depending on your use of air conditioning and the size of your living space.

Cooking gas costs between $6 and $25 per tank, depending on the size. There is a one-time charge for the bottle and gas is delivered free (and promptly) with just a phone call, even on holidays. We once ran out of gas during a Khmer holiday and the delivery man showed up at our door 20 minutes later with a fresh bottle on his shoulder.

International Shipping Of Goods

Shipping stuff to Cambodia is not cheap - and sometimes doesn't arrive.

When we left home, we shipped a box to ourselves (to be delivered to our guesthouse) which was costly and didn't arrive for more than four weeks. After waiting and watching for it, we were told to go to the central post office (near Wat Phnom) to check the book that lists packages arriving in Phnom Penh which hadn't been delivered. It turned out the box had arrived two days after we did, and because it hadn't been delivered and had been "stored" at the post office, we had to pay another fee to get it out again.

When you go to the post office to find your package, you'll have to sift through a book listing every box or mailer shipped to Cambodia to find your name, then point it out to the postal employee who will head into the storage area to exhume your stuff.

We've often heard from friends who have sent books and other packages that never arrived, so I'm reluctant to have anything mailed to Cambodia through the postal service. If someone ships you a packet through the mail, make sure to get the tracking code so you can track it online to see when it arrives. FedEx, UPS, and DHL, though costly, are completely reliable. Also keep in mind that the post office is very particular on addresses and if your postage is missing a "khan" (district) on the "chamkarmon" (name of the khan), you might not get a notice that it has arrived.

For larger items, such as furniture and artwork, there are shipping companies which send to Cambodia and are quite dependable. It's best to check with your home country, and do the footwork before you leave.

In Phnom Penh, there are several international shipping companies to choose from:

DHL - Worldwide Express
#353, Street 110
Tel: +855 (0)23-427726
FedEx
#701D, Monivong
Tel: +855 (0)23-216712

TNT
#28, Monivong
Tel: + 855 (0)23-430922
UPS
#27, Street 134
Tel: +855 (0)23-427511

Jobs Available For Foreigners

Many foreigners come to Cambodia to teach English or volunteer as an easy way of getting a foothold in the country. There are, however, lots of opportunities once you're here, and my husband and I have had work dropping into our laps in our fields (writing and marketing) without looking for them.

The main place for foreigners to find jobs is in development work. Cambodia has the second highest number of NGOs in the world (after Rwanda), and there are often jobs for foreigners with experience in relief work, economics, arbitration, advocacy, or other technical or highly-skilled work, since few Cambodians specialise in this sector. There are also jobs for foreigners teaching in various educational institutions as well as in computer programming, sales, and the hospitality industry.

Bear in mind that salaries are much lower here than in the western world, but the cost of living is also much lower than most other countries and companies will generally help in obtaining work permits.

Work Permits

According to Cambodian law, foreigners are meant to get work permits.

There are many people, however, who have worked here for years without them and most aren't even aware that such a thing exists. According to a local law firm, the Ministry of Labour and Vocational Training is striving to impose compliance, which is mainly done on a voluntary basis, and authorities are cracking down more and more on foreign workers who don't have a permit.

In order to get one, you'll need to visit the Ministry office which is located at #3, Russian Federation Boulevard in Phnom Penh to obtain applications forms (take your passport, Cambodian visa, and two passport-sized photos and a $100 fee). They also request an "employment contract in Khmer" and a health check at the health department. They do not presently have a website and their phone number is + 855 (0) 12 819 679.

For a more in depth summary, check :
http://www.mekongmigration.org/labourlaw/index.php?option=com_content&view=article&id=149:cambodia&catid=57:section-12&Itemid=96

Finding Work

As with many other things in Cambodia, the best way to find a job is by being on the ground and networking. LinkedIn is also a great resource, as there are a number of groups worth joining where you can start to network online before even arriving. Among those are Cambodia Professionals, Cambodia Private Sector, Cambodia Creative Hub, Cambodian Center for Human Rights, NGO Professionals for Southeast Asia, International Development, Expat Careers, Cambodia Business Network, and Invest In Cambodia.

For person-to-person networking, there are a number of professional organisations worth checking out in Phnom Penh:

International Business Chamber of Cambodia

Tel: +855 (0)23 210 225 / 362 670
http://www.ibccambodia.com

American Cambodian Business Council
www.amchamcambodia.net

Australian Business Association Cambodia
Monthly lunches on the second Wednesday of each month.
awcphn@gmail.com
http://www.australianbusinessasia.org

Cambodian Chamber of Commerce
Building No.7D, Russian Blvd
Tel: +855 (0)23 880 795
http://www.ccc.org.kh

European Chamber of Commerce in Cambodia
10th floor, Phnom Penh Tower, #445 Monivong Blvd
Tel: +855 (0)10 801 950
http://eurocham-cambodia.org

British Business Association of Cambodia
http://www.bbacambodia.com

Phnom Penh Chamber of Commerce
Building No.7D, Russian Blvd.
info@ppcc.org.kh
Tel: +855 (0)23 880 795
http://www.ppcc.org.kh

Chambre de Commerce Franco-Cambodgienne
33 E2 Sothearos Blvd.
Tel: +855 (0)23-221453
ccfc@online.com.kh
www.ccfcambodge.org

German Business Group of Cambodia
No. 113, 3FDE Parkway Square, Mao Tse Toung Blvd

Malaysian Business Council of Cambodia (BCC)
Holiday Villa, 89 Monivong Blvd

Tel: + 855 (0)16 836 222
mbcc.secretariat@gmail.com

Here are some useful Cambodian websites for foreign job seekers to use when seeking employment in Cambodia:

http://www.phnompenhpost.com
www.camhr.com
www.bongthom.com
www.hrcambodia.com
www.pelprek.com
www.cambodiajobpage.com

Travel Insurance

If you're planning on spending time and investing resources in Cambodia, it's a good idea to have insurance that will cover you for medical necessities and emergencies, evacuation, and maybe even for property if you own valuable furnishings. A recent newspaper article told the story of an expat living in Cambodia who had a heart attack and discovered her insurance had run out. Her family was doing all they could to raise money to get her back to her homeland as she was unable to afford it herself, but in the meantime, she was stranded and helpless.

This is an extreme case but it brings home the importance of being covered by insurance. There are many companies offering policies which cover the basics, as well as just emergency coverage, and include the following:

- Asia Insurance   http://www.asiainsurance.com.kh
- Caminco   http://www.caminco.com.kh
- Forte Insurance   http://www.forteinsurance.com
- Global Surance   http://www.globalsurance.com
- World Nomads   http://www.worldnomads.com
- Global Insurance   http://www.globalhealthinsurance.com/
- Infinity Insurance   http://www.infinity.com.kh

Pricing for expat health insurance is cheaper than health insurance in most western countries. In the US, my husband and I were paying $1,000 per month on COBRA after we left our jobs. Here, we were quoted less than $5,000 per *year* for the two of us (and included evacuation insurance). Talk to an insurance broker in Cambodia who will offer you the best option for your needs.

Educational Opportunities

There are a number of primary and secondary schools for expats which have good reputations. Since there are many foreigners moving into the country, the demand for quality international education is starting to exceed supply, and some of the schools have waiting lists.

Education is extremely important to Cambodians, and anyone who can afford to is taking classes to improve their station in life. Many of my Cambodian colleagues take classes in English, marketing, or business on the weekends. We've spoken with young waiters who are attending university at the same time as working in restaurants. One of our tuktuk drivers takes English, Korean, and driving classes when he scrapes together enough money to do so.

While many schools use the word "international" in their name, it doesn't necessarily mean anything (there's even one called the

American Idol International School). There are three real international schools in Phnom Penh: ISPP, iCAN, and Northbridge. iCAN is a British international school which also follows the International Primary Curriculum (IPC). ISPP follows the International *Baccalaureate* (IB) curriculum, as does Northbridge.

These are some of the top choices:

Hope International School
No. 239-243, Street 271,
Tel : +855 (0)23- 217565 +855 (0)78-210320 (Siem Reap)
www.hopeschool-cambodia.org

ICAN British International School
International pre-school - Grade 6
No. 85, Sothearos Blvd.
Tel: +855 (0)23-222416
www.ican.edu.kh

International School of Phnom Penh (ISPP)
International pre-school - Grade 12
No. 146, Norodom Blvd.
Tel: +855 (0)23-213103
www.ispp.edu.kh

Lycée Française René Descartes de Phnom Penh
http://www.descartes-cambodge.com

Northbridge International School Cambodia (NISC)
International pre-school - Grade 12
Northbridge Road
Tel: +855 (0)23-886000
http://www.nisc.edu.kh

Zaman International School
No.39, Street 315, Tuol Kork
Tel: +855 (0)23-884040
http://zamanisc.com

Preschools:

Cambridge Child Development Center
(Pre-school)
No.21A, Street 302
Tel: +855 (0)16-499599
www.cambridgecdc.net

Gecko & Garden Pre-School
No. 3, Street 21
Tel: +855 (0)92-57543; +855 (0)23-214568
http://www.geckogarden-preschool.org

Phnom Penh Montessori International Day Care and Pre-School (PPMI)
No. 106, Russian Blvd.
Tel +855 (0)97-7779987

Raffles Montessori International
No.18, Street 294 (Corner of St. 57)
Tel: +855 (0) 23- 993999
http://www.rmispp.edu.kh

Sambo's Tots Playhouse & Playschool
No.14, Street 398
Tel: +855 (0)23-211044
http://www.sambostots.com

The Giving Tree
No. 17 Street 71
Tel: +855 (0)17-997 112
http://www.thegivingtreeschool.com

Tree and Garden International School
No. 76, Street 57
Tel: +855 (0)23-6373056
http://www.tgiscambodia.com

Things To Buy Before You Arrive

Before we came to Cambodia, we thought we'd have to stock up and on things we wouldn't be able to find.

Wrong. Almost everything we thought would be missing was available. Even some of the prescription meds we brought with us were readily available here, most of them at a fraction of the cost and some which didn't even require a prescription.

The only things I'd suggest buying would be brand name items you can't live without. For example, my husband can't get a particular brand of contact lens solution, and I have friends who use specific skin care products or perfumes that they can't find here. I also have a friend with a child who has food allergies and is unable to find anything for their restricted diets (such as sunflower butter, instant oatmeal, and snack bars).

It's also good to have a good umbrella and shoes that fare well in waterlogged conditions, since you'll definitely be wading through ankle deep water many times during rainy season.

You might also want to stock up on underwear if you're on the larger side, since the Cambodian body-type is slender and much smaller than the western shape.

There's a section on the Expat Advisory website entitled "Hard to find items" which is helpful if you're looking for something specific such as marshmallows, mould killer, cookie cutters, or animal manure (actual posts on the site).

Things You Wish You Had Brought

Once we started buying house goods for our new apartment, we discovered that Cambodian bedding is not up to the same standard as it is in the western world. Sheets have a seam down the middle, blankets don't quite reach the end of the bed (not that you ever need them) and pillows are lumpier than I like them. Towels also pose a challenge, as they are mostly cheap and non-absorbent. If you can fit them in, bring them with you. In fact, bring lots of them, since almost every expat in town is hungry for a good pair of soft pillows and a silky sheet.

Things You Wish You Had Left Home

The only things I wish I'd left home are clothes that are heavier than long–sleeved cotton shirts or light slacks. My sweatshirts are still sitting in the bottom of the suitcase two years after arrival, and warm socks have become collector's items. Nevertheless, they are good to have for trips to northern Vietnam or Laos where the temperatures actually do fall below 70 (or for when your blood thins so much that you want to wear a warm jacket, like the locals).

It's also not necessary to have formal clothing, since everything is ultra-casual. The only time this may be necessary is if you're working in a corporate environment or intend to spend time at Raffles or symphony concerts at the Intercontinental. Cambodian weddings also provide an opportunity to don the heels and glittery tops (not so for men, who are accepted in casual attire). Otherwise, casual trousers, a nice top (or collared shirt for men), and a good pair of sandals constitutes formal clothing.

Living There

Cambodia is a country of exquisite contrasts. One minute you'll find yourself sitting on a rooftop cocktail bar drinking cosmopolitans, and the next you'll be squatting on a plastic chair in the street eating grilled eggs (*pongmuang ang*) with the locals. On the way to work, you'll often pass a couple of chickens scratching in the dirt next to a chauffeur-driven Lexus SUV and, on your way home, will see a brilliant orange sunset over a pagoda, while a dirty barefoot child sleeps under his tarpaulin home on the street.

Etiquette

Before we came to Cambodia, we read a lot about the customs and traditions of the local people but discovered upon living here that, as foreigners, we're mostly given a hall-pass when it comes to knowing the right things to do.

However, there are certain lines that even a foreigner should not cross. There's a huge respect for anything to do with religion or seniors (either in age or in status), and it's important not to show disregard for things that are culturally significant.

Deference must always be shown to the most senior person; and when meeting a group of Khmer, you will first be introduced to the highest ranking person. If groups are involved, you should introduce people according to rank, so that your Cambodian counterparts understand the dynamics of the group.

Handshakes are normal, although a very firm shake may be construed as aggressive. When in mixed company, a man should wait and see if the woman extends a hand before doing so.

The traditional Cambodian "sampeah" (two hands held together as if in prayer) is done as a sign of respect upon meeting someone for the first time, as well as to more senior people (along with the words *"chumreap sua"* meaning hello), and also upon saying goodbye (*"chumreap lia"* meaning goodbye). When entering someone's house (and sometimes office), it is customary to take off your shoes, and it's respectful to wear conservative clothing when visiting a pagoda or religious place.

There's a hierarchy and way of greeting for different age groups which is confusing to figure out. An older man, for example, is referred to as "pu" (uncle), while a man around your own age or a little older is called "bong" (brother or sister) or "lok" (mister), and a younger male would be called "own." And everyone, whether related or not, is a "sister," "brother," "uncle," or "aunty."

However, unlike most other cultures, most Khmers do not celebrate birthdays and many older people may not even know the date of their birth - so you may be on your own to figure out their age.

Names are written in reverse of how they are written in the west. So, a person with the name Kim Ngounteang has a first name of Ngounteang (usually abbreviated to Teang) and his last name is Kim. It's considered rude to call him Mr. Kim since that's his family name, and the right way to address him is Mr. Teang (or "bong Teang" or "pu Teang"—depending on his age). Or just Teang.

Expressions of anger are rarely (if ever) shown, as Cambodians tend to laugh off uncomfortable or confrontational situations. Showing emotion is considered a negative behaviour and should be hidden, as it would lead to a loss of face. It's not uncommon to see people laugh when dealing with traffic accidents, workplace conflicts, and personal frustrations.

There aren't many boundaries in Cambodian culture and it's quite normal to be asked how old you are, how much you weigh, or how much you pay for your rent. It's also common to find a work colleague staring over your shoulder into your computer screen as you email your husband or saying something like "You look fat today," or "Why you sweat so much?" It's just normal curiosity for them and may take some time getting used to.

If you're a woman, you'll be asked if you have children, since Cambodians place a huge value on family. If you don't, you'll probably be met with expressions of sympathy.

One of the things that strikes me most about Cambodian people is that they have an incredibly childlike disposition. It's normal to see a group of young men playing ball on a street corner, children playing outside in torrential rainstorms, or businessmen teasing one another in a work setting. And there's a level of graciousness and appreciation which continues to impress.

We were once told about a westerner visiting the home of a Cambodian who noticed their young son kicking a sandal around the street with a group of friends.

"Isn't it sad he doesn't have a ball to play with," commented the westerner.

"I don't see it that way at all," said his mother. "I think it's wonderful that he has so many friends to play with."

In keeping with the lack of personal boundaries, Cambodians also demonstrate outward signs of physical affection. You'll often see two young women holding hands or a couple of men with their arms around one another. If you find yourself being touched or hugged, understand this is a sign of affection and acceptance, and that there's nothing sexual or improper about it.

There are also a number of personal habits which may be alarming to visitors from the west. Everywhere you look, you'll see men urinating on walls or trees, and Cambodians think nothing of picking their nose or spitting onto the street in public.

We've also encountered forms of reverse discrimination which made us feel awkward. Once, my husband and I attended a large conference featuring speakers and attendees from around the country. When the organiser spotted us, she hurried to the door and ushered us to the VIP seats in the front row, simply because we are westerners, even though she had no idea who we were. We were there as volunteers representing the NGOs we worked for, and it made us feel uncomfortable to be given prime seating while our more senior colleagues sat at the back of the room.

Another time, we were attending the Water Festival celebrations in Phnom Penh, where a couple of million people descended on the city. While walking along the riverside, we came upon a large tented area with seats facing the finishing post for the races. It was reserved "For Foreigners." We decided to keep walking as it felt wrong to us – as guests in this country – that we should be encouraged to occupy prominent comfortable positions when everyone else had to stand outside in the blistering heat.

Since Cambodia is an extremely poor country, there are likely to be a number of disturbing sights you'll encounter while walking around the towns. Landmine victims often beg for money or sell handcrafted items, tiny brown-eyed children loiter in touristy areas selling photocopied books or jasmine wreaths, and impoverished families sometimes live in corrugated cardboard shelters on the street. While a small number of street people may be scam artists, we've found most of them to be legitimately unfortunate Cambodians who are struggling to eke out a day's living. Giving money to children is discouraged (like in "Oliver Twist," there's usually a Fagin running the scheme), but we often give to handicapped, blind, or impoverished people who receive no support from anywhere else.

As an example of the heartbreakingly incongruous, there's a disfigured man with no legs who sits on the riverfront every day with a bathroom scale, offering people the opportunity to weigh themselves for a small tip. Whenever we pass him by, we drop some money into his box without using his services. Chances are, you'll find similar cases that you can't resist helping.

When it comes to giving, we are often humbled by Cambodians, as we'll often see our tuktuk driver or work colleague putting his hand into his pocket and giving a handful of bills to a beggar. The Buddhist philosophy of doing good in preparation for the next life is constantly present and, even when they don't have money themselves, people tend to help their fellow countrymen with open hearts.

In the rural parts of Cambodia (as well as in more local regions of the towns), you'll generally be regarded as a fascinating anomaly since many villagers rarely, if ever, see westerners. You will be stared at and smiled at, and small children often run away in fear at seeing a large white person in their village. If you're cycling or driving through the countryside, though, one of the sweetest things is hearing tiny voices shouting "hello" as little children run out to wave and practice the only word of English they know. Make sure you wave back, as it will make their day.

In the markets, haggling is expected, but don't expect vendors to drop prices too much (particularly in touristy areas). You can also bargain for better deals if you're staying for a lengthy time in a guesthouse or hotel, as well as taking tours.

Cambodians love it when you speak their language, even if it's only a few words and everyone, without exception, will comment on how well you speak Khmer (even if you only say "thank you").

Tipping

When we first came to Cambodia, we were told it was not customary to tip. However, I discovered differently after going to lunch with a group of Cambodian colleagues, when the administrative assistant pulled out her wallet after the meal.

"People in my country don't have much money," she said, as she dropped a couple of bills on the table.

Since this gesture came from a young woman making less than $400 per month, we now leave a tip wherever we go. It's usually only a dollar or two, depending on the amount of the bill (or you can just round up to the nearest dollar).

Tipping is also considerate when getting a massage or other beauty service, as well as any other place where a service has been rendered (such as delivery of gas or food to your home, tour guides, and hotel staff).

Toilets

Bathrooms in Cambodia are very different to those in the western world. While the expat places (hotels, restaurants, cafes, etc) all have western-style toilets, many of the more local establishments may not.

I always make sure to keep a few tissues in my pocket when I'm travelling, since buses usually stop at places with squat toilets which never have toilet paper. And many of the smaller hotels and eating places have less than desirable facilities. I've waded through mud patches in the rain to get to outdoor toilets, as well as walked past chicken and pigs to reach a bathroom.

Even in cities, you'll find local restaurants with simple toilets, many of which require you to throw tissue into a bin instead of down the toilet due to bad plumbing. Almost every bathroom in Cambodia comes equipped with a spray hose which is a small nozzle attached to a hose to the side of the toilet – used as a replacement for toilet paper – and the "flush" mechanism is often a plastic bucket which should be filled with water and thrown into the squat loo.

Expat Social Clubs & Networking

There are many types of expats in Cambodia, each of which have their own social scene (some of which overlap).

There's the backpacker, the NGO worker or volunteer, the corporate expat, the office worker, and the retiree (and, of course, the unsavoury types who linger around the girly bars).

For every group there are a number of activities, from quiz nights to show jumping events, happy hours and human rights' talks, cycling clubs to salsa classes. Sometimes they are not easy to find - and it's only through meeting people, discovering them online, joining the

Cambodian Parents' Network, or reading about upcoming events - that you might unearth them.

There are a number of free magazines listing places to go and things to do, which include *AsiaLife, LeBoost, Bayon Pearnik, The Advisor,* and *the Pocket Guides (Out & About in Phnom Penh and Siem Reap, Drinking & Dining Phnom Penh, Siem Reap* and *Phnom Penh After Dark).*

When it comes to social clubs, there aren't a lot of visible ones since people tend to put together their own little groups with like-minded people (readers, bikers, movie buffs, runners, and more).

Here are some worth knowing about:

Women's International Group

A social group for women which holds monthly meetings on the first Wednesday of the month at 10am in the Intercontinental Hotel, as well as bridge, tennis, coffee mornings, mahjong, cocktail functions, and social events.

http://www.wigcambodia.com

Australian Connection: Women's Social Group
Tel: +855 (0)12 812291, +855 (0)12-800312
awcphn@gmail.com

Phnom Penh Accueil, a French speaking social network

Meets weekly at Kwest restaurant on Sisowath Quay every Friday, from 8:30am to 12:pm. Includes numerous activities such as walks around Phnom Penh on Thursdays with an emphasis on cultural sites, Pilates and aquagym classes, book club, sewing classes, and social events.

http://phnom-penh-accueil.org

Rotary Club Phnom Penh
Meets each Friday at 12:15 at Kanji restaurant (128F Sothearos Boulevard, next to the Almond Hotel).
http://www.rotaryclubpp.org/
rotaryphnompenh@gmail.com
Tel: +855 (0)15 628 495

Online newspapers and magazines
Phnom Penh Post – PhnomPenhPost.com
Southeast Asia Globe – SeaGlobe.com
AsiaLife Guide - AsiaLifeGuide.com
Voice of America (for Cambodia) - voacambodia.com
Bayon Pearknik – BayonPearknik.com

Food

Food is a focal point for most Cambodians. A typical greeting, after saying *"Sua s'day"* (hello), is often *"Nyam baai howee?"* which means "Have you eaten?" – and the word for eat (*"nyam baai"*) literally translates into "eat rice," showing the importance of that staple dish in everyone's life.

For a population which is so tiny and slight, Cambodians manage to consume enormous amounts of rice. A meal isn't a meal without it - for breakfast, lunch, and dinner. Meals are social events and it's a wonderful experience (and honour) to be invited to the home of a Cambodian to see how they eat and socialise.

While there is an extraordinary number of Cambodian *hangbais* (small streetside restaurants), beer gardens, and markets selling local food, a westerner need not be concerned about missing out on anything from home. You'll find French, Italian, Indian, Chinese, Russian, American, Mediterranean, and any number of other cuisines available in the numerous restaurants in the main cities – as well as some of the best breads around, courtesy of the French who left behind some of their signatures after departing the country. There are places with world-class cakes, imported oysters, and handmade Belgian chocolates, as well as restaurants serving sushi, Australian lamb, and fish and chips. There is a welcome absence from most western fast-food chains, with the exception of KFC, Dairy Queen and Swensen's Ice Cream, which were the first fast food places to open in Cambodia in 2007, as well as a few Asian chains such as

114

Lucky Burger, Pizza Company, and one newly opened Burger King, which is, so far, only at Phnom Penh's airport.

Traditional Cambodian food is influenced by a number of cultures, including Thai (though less spicy), Vietnamese (both sharing the French colonial history), Chinese (with variations of rice noodles), and Indian (curries).

A typical Cambodian meal consists of three or four courses and generally includes soup (*samlor*). You'll usually find dishes of peanuts sprinkled with salt (and sometimes sugar) on the tables in Cambodian restaurants as well as the signature bowls of fresh chillies, soy sauce, and pickled spicy vegetables.

In big cities, you'll find a number of upscale Cambodian restaurants (some of which even offer tarantula on the menu), but in the villages and small towns you'll be hard pressed to find anything that resembles western food (although you'll generally find eggs and the ubiquitous French fries).

You will, however, find an interesting array of snack foods, including deep-fried crickets, fertilised duck eggs (with the embryo inside), snakes on skewers, and termites.

My husband was once given a couple of crickets by his Cambodian workmates and bravely popped them into his mouth before learning you're meant to take the legs off first. He actually found them quite tasty and said they tasted like roasted nuts, only crunchier.

Skuon, a village around 55 miles north of Phnom Penh, is colloquially known as "Spiderville," as it's the home of the fried black spider (a delicacy dating back to the dark days of the Khmer Rouge rule when residents were forced to eat spiders out of desperation – and took a liking to it).

While you may not be craving spiders, the best way to get a taste of Cambodia is to eat in a local restaurant. Learn a few words of Khmer so you know what you're ordering - or take a chance and point to something on the menu. You'll always find fried pork, a selection of vegetables, including the ubiquitous morning glory (a water plant with a thick hollow stem tasting a little like spinach), chicken (which is usually full of bones and not very meaty), fish dishes (usually fried, with spices such as lemongrass, garlic, and chilli), and piles of rice with everything. Beef is comparatively expensive and usually cut into small pieces, which may be tough and chewy, and mixed with vegetables. I've been to places where there's not much that appealed to me so I've pushed aside the main courses, covered my rice with sauce and a few chillies, added some vegetables, and made a meal out of it. It's worth it for the experience.

Many of the smaller places won't even have menus, as they are often frequented by regulars from the village or only offer a couple of

117

specific dishes that they specialise in. In some towns, there are places which are packed at 7am because they only serve breakfast - fried pork and rice (*bai saw saich chrouk*), noodle soup (*khtieau*), rice porridge *(bobor)*, or noodles *(mee cha)* - and others which offer a selection of lunch dishes in open chafing dishes that you can point to and be served. In places like this, main courses don't usually cost more than $2.

It's the same in the local markets. From early morning, food vendors are frying, boiling, stirring, and sautéing all kinds of delicious dishes, which cost between 50 cents and $2 for a plate. Crispy fried chive rice cakes (*nom kachay)* served with a spicy sauce are delicious, as are *ban chao* (thin crisp pancakes filled with bean sprouts and your choice of ground meat and vegetables and eaten with a selection of greens). You may also find stir-fried noodles, soups, deep-fried fish, animal stomachs, barbequed squid, spring rolls, and rice dishes.

Then there's the ever-present dessert. Cambodians love sweet things and every market offers a selection of sugary treats, since the most popular times for dessert are mid-morning (while the women are doing their grocery shopping), mid-afternoon, and evening. You may not recognise them as desserts since they are usually presented in a collection of shiny silver bowls and may consist of gelatinous, colourful balls or blobs made from semolina or rice flour and covered with coconut cream, condensed milk, shaved ice, and palm sugar. There are also fried bananas (usually consumed as an afternoon snack), waffles made with coconut cream, sticky rice wrapped around a fruit or bean, and fried doughnuts.

You'll also find a wonderful selection of exotic fruit (and fruit juice) in almost every spot you visit. Mangos, mangosteen, rambutan, dragon fruit, lychees, rose apples, pomelo, guava, and langan are among them. Funnily enough, one of the preferred ways to serve fruit is to dip it into a mix of salt and chillies -it's a delicious combination but a strange way of making something healthy into something not so healthy.

Then there's the "king of fruit" – the durian – which you either love or hate. Banned from many hotels because of its foul odour, this enormous fruit is well-known in Cambodia and worth tasting if you can get beyond the dirty-sock smell. For many it's an acquired taste. The flavour was described by 19th century British naturalist, Alfred Russell Wallace, as "a rich custard highly flavoured with almonds, but there are occasional wafts of flavour that call to mind cream cheese, onion sauce, sherry wine and other incongruous dishes."

Another "love it or hate it" aromatic ingredient in Cambodian cuisine is *prahok* (nicknamed "Cambodian cheese"), which is fermented fish paste used as a seasoning or a condiment. It's often served with fried chicken or vegetables as a dip, tossed into soup, or mixed with meat. One thing's for sure: you'll know by the sour smell coming from the kitchen when it's in your meal.

There are a number of regional specialties, the best known being Kep crab, which are among the tastiest crab you'll have anywhere. They are caught by the hundreds every day off the coast and sold in the local crab market, as well as in restaurants throughout the area. I've heard of people driving from Phnom Penh to Kep for lunch (almost a three-hour drive) because they had a craving for crab. Add to it the world-famous fresh pepper grown in neighbouring Kampot, and you have a winner.

Fish is popular in most areas of the country since the Tonle Sap Lake is the second biggest source of freshwater fish in the world after the Amazon, providing many types, which are fried, sautéed, grilled, barbecued, served with garlic and sauces, and used in soups.

Meals are eaten with a spoon and a fork (the spoon in the right hand), and napkins are tossed on the floor in most local casual eating spots, along with chicken bones and any other disposable items.

Many Cambodian dishes are served with a fried egg on top and usually accompanied by a selection of spicy sauces. *Kroeung* is a complex spice blend made from lemongrass, shallots, cilantro, kaffir lime leaves, galangal, and garlic, and is frequently a main ingredient in many local dishes.

While almost all dishes contain rice or noodles, there are a few specialties which pop up on most Cambodian menus:

Amok Trei (Fish Amok): One of Cambodia's signature dishes, fish amok is a dish of steamed curried fish seasoned with coconut milk, lemongrass, turmeric powder, paprika, garlic, ginger, and fish sauce - either steamed or baked in a cup made from banana leaves. You'll also see variations on menus, such as chicken amok or vegetable amok.

Beef Lok Lak: Another famous Cambodian dish, beef lok lak consists of cubes of stir-fried beef served with onions and tomato slices on a bed of fresh lettuce, dipped in a salt and pepper lime sauce with a fried egg on top.

K'tieu: Mostly served for breakfast, this is a traditional pork-based noodle soup garnished with fresh bean sprouts, chopped scallions, and cilantro (and sometimes eaten with fried breadsticks known as *cha-kwai* at breakfast).

Borbor: A type of congee or rice porridge which can be plain or include chicken or pork and served with fresh bean sprouts and green onions. Borbor is often served at breakfast or in the evening, and can also be a dessert dish containing fruits, such as bananas or jackfruit, instead of meat.

Pleah: Partially cooked beef or shrimp in a salad flavoured with prahok and tossed with onions and fresh herbs in a sauce of lime juice, fish sauce, Vietnamese mint, and peanuts.

Bok Lahong: A tasty salad made from papaya, dried shrimp, and peanuts drenched in a vinegary dressing.

Num Banh Chop: Piles of noodles served with fish, coconut paste, and heaps of raw herbs, chillies, and veggies topped with a fragrant combination of lemongrass, galangal, fish sauce, and coconut with a peanut-based broth.

Somlor Machu Kreung: Cambodian pork rib and beef tendon braised coconut soup with water spinach, lemon grass paste, and ripe tamarind in a combination of nutty and tangy flavours.

Cha knyei: A spicy dish of meat stir fried with lots of ginger root, black pepper, and chilies.

Ngam nguv: Chicken soup flavoured with whole preserved lemons.

Sach Ko Ang: Literally translated into "grilled beef," this dish is an appetizer of beef skewers flavoured with lemongrass.

There are also a number of interesting snack dishes sold by street vendors which include:

Kralan: Bamboo tubes filled with sticky rice, coconut milk, and black beans cooked over charcoal and sold bundled together by street vendors.

Chook: Seeds of the lotus flower, which are sold in bundles of three or five heads so you can pop out the seeds, peel them, and eat them like garden peas.

The cheapest food in Cambodia is found on the street – whether it's from a pushcart vendor selling grilled bananas and grilled chicken skewers, or from a sidewalk food stand where you'll sit on a small plastic chair at a short metal table and dine on grilled eggs (*pongmuang ang*) or stir-fried noodles. You'll often spend less than a couple of dollars for a full meal and have a more local experience than in any restaurant.

You can also get food delivered from many of the western-style restaurants around town if you don't feel like venturing out in a rainstorm or want a lazy night at home. Pick up a copy of *"Door to Door"* which lists all the options. Delivery is free, but it's advisable to give a tip to the delivery person.

And if you'd like to prepare dishes at home, there are cooking classes where you can learn how to cook Cambodian food and construct bowls made from banana leaves to hold your *fish amok.*

Drinking Water

It's always best to drink bottled or boiled water in Cambodia. Although water from the tap is said to be fine, the piping and added chlorine make it not so fine. We spent our first year boiling water before investing in a water filter, which is inexpensive and can be found in various shops around the Central Market.

Alternately, you can buy a water cooler with a refillable five-gallon jug and have bottled water delivered to your home. There are a number of companies around, such as Eurotech, Hi Tech, and Mother that provide this service. Just look around for bottles in your local grocery store, as they will have a phone number on them that you can call for delivery. Cost is $4 for the initial bottle deposit and $1 for every five-gallon bottle delivered.

You'll also want to be careful about ice in local restaurants, particularly at street stalls or in the villages. Ice is produced in large cubes which are delivered to outlets and shops and you'll often see people hacking away with pickaxes at large slabs of ice in back alleys so they can use it for cooling or pop it into your drink. Rule of thumb is if you get **chunks of ice** in your drink, it's probably not safe. If you get **nicely rounded cubes** with holes in them, it's fine.

Tap water in the countryside (if available) **should be avoided** altogether, as the source and treatment of the water is not always clear. Brushing your teeth with tap water is fine.

Cost Of Everyday Things

When you buy groceries from supermarkets, you'll find prices are generally less than what you pay in the western world, mysteriously so when it comes to brand names like Ritz crackers. We prefer to buy produce from local, outdoor markets as it costs less than half and there's an abundance of freshly-grown and picked fruits and veggies. Make sure to wash everything well before eating, though (tap water is fine to use for rinsing).

The main supermarkets include Pencil, Lucky, and Bayon in Phnom Penh; the prices below reflect purchases made in these markets.

Loaf of bread: $1.20

Liter of milk: $2

Packet of breakfast cereal: $4.50 (brand Cornflakes); $2.45 (non brand)

1.5 liter bottle of water: 30 cents

One can of beer from supermarket: 45 cents

A beer from an expat-type bar: $1.50

Fancy dinner for two: $30 will get you a really good meal in a nice western restaurant with drinks.

Cheap dinner for two: You can get a great meal in some of the local *hang bais* (small restaurants), beer gardens, and Chinese dumpling houses for less than $10 for two, with drinks. At a local Cambodian market or street side food stand, you can get two meals for less than $5.

Apples: $2.50/kg

Carrots: $1.10/kg

Head of lettuce: 25 cents

Tomatoes: $1/kg

Mangoes: $1.10/kg (50c/kg from a street vendor)

A hand of bananas: $1

1kg pork: $8 for pork loin

1kg chicken: $4.50 for chicken breast

1kg beef: $9

Block of tofu: 45 cents

Packet of cat food: $2.35 (480g packet of Whiskas)

Six-packet of toilet paper (two-ply): $1.50

Tin of infant formula: $5 for 400g

Single serve tub of yoghurt: 30 cents

Bowl of noodles: $1 for a bowl of noodles covered in chopped taro spring rolls at the Russian market

Can of Coca-Cola: 25 cents

Burger from a fast-food joint: $1.30

Home delivered family pizza: $6 - $8 for medium-large pizza from Nike Pizza (plus tip)

1kg rice: from $1 - $3.90 (depending on the type of rice)

500 g packet of laundry powder: 95 cents

Bottle of fish sauce: $1.95 (750 ml)

Tube of toothpaste: $1.20 (Colgate)

Packet of tampons: $3.40 for 16

Packet of sanitary napkins: $2 for 18

Packet of condoms: $2 for 2

Packet of pasta: $1.50

Bottle of ready-made pasta sauce: $4.20 (730g Ragu)

Bottle of wine: $10 (Wyndham Estate chardonnay)

Packet of fancy crackers: $3.05

Imported fancy cheese: $6.30 (18 oz goat cheese)

Plastic wrap: $2.30

1kg of flour: $3.50

Bottle of shampoo: $1.50 (non brand)

A dozen eggs: $1.20

Litre of petrol: $1.40

There are also many smaller markets in Phnom Penh where you can buy good (and sometimes harder-to-find) items. They include:

The Food Pantry: No. 25Z, Street 105 and 42, Street 178.

Thai Hout: No. 99-105 Monivong Boulevard.

Veggy's: No. 23, Street 240.

Natural Garden: No. 213B, Street 63 (near Street 322).

Dan Meats: No. 51A, Street 214.

Le Duo deli: No. 17, Street 228.

Comme a la Maison French deli: No. 15, Street 57 (near Street 294).

Chocolate by The Shop: 317 Street 63, between St 322 and 334.

Other costs of daily life in Cambodia include the following:

Housecleaner: We pay $45 for a cleaner to clean our two-bedroom apartment once a week, and have friends who pay $120 per month for full time work (five days a week). Sometimes the housecleaner will also cook for the family.

Nanny: Between $175 and $300 per month (full time).

This website will provide guidance if you want to hire someone to work in your home, as well as learn about guidelines for employment in Cambodia: Prake.org/home.

When you're looking for places to shop, there are a number of options around Phnom Penh. My favourite places to go are the local markets where you can get a great cultural experience as well as pick up almost everything you need.

The most comprehensive (and overwhelming) is **Orrussey Market** – an enormous multi-tiered covered market which sells everything from bicycle parts to sequinned fabrics to bed linens, pots and pans, bathroom fittings, and clothing. There are also dozens of food vendors crammed into the steamy aisles, some sautéing noodles over a burner and others carrying trays of sticky rice desserts on their heads or around their necks.

The **Russian Market** is more comfortable and tourist-oriented (while Orrussey is more of a local place for everything). It is on the south side of town and great for buying good-quality bootleg DVDs ($1.50 each), shimmering silk table runners and hangings, carved Buddhas, cheap clothing, and attractive souvenirs. As with every local market, there's a selection of food places where you can get a tasty meal, cooked fresh for less than $2.

Central Market is somewhere between the above-mentioned two. It's not as crowded or overwhelming as Orrussey and still good for finding a wide range of stuff. And **Olympic Market** is similar to Central Market, as well as having the best selection of fabric vendors.

Every Friday, Saturday, and Sunday evening from 5pm to midnight, there's a **Night Market** (located at the north end at the riverside) where you can find souvenirs, food, clothing, and knickknacks, as well as listen to live Cambodian entertainment.

Shopping malls aren't like those back home but there are a couple which are fun to browse in and most of them have large supermarkets on the ground level. Check out the **Sorya Mall, Sovanna Mall,** and **Bayon Malls** around town (Bayon has a good kitchen shop on the top level).

When it comes to fresh produce, we usually buy ours at open air markets, such as Psaar Kandal (located a block off the riverfront between Streets 136 and 154), BKK market (Street 63, between Street 380 and Street 392), or Psaar Chas (between Streets 110 and 108). Here you can buy good quality fruit and vegetables at a fraction of supermarket costs and get a hefty dose of local flavour at the same time.

For **specialty shopping**, there are a couple of streets much frequented by expats.

Street 240 is home to a handful of nice boutiques selling silks, art, fashions, and furniture, and **Street 178** is known as "art street," since there are a number of art galleries and sculpture shops along the route.

For books, **Monument Books** on Norodom (near Street 240) has the largest selection of new books in their comfortable air-conditioned space, while Boston Books (Street 240), D's Books (Street 240), and Bohr's Books (Street 172) sell a wide range of used books.

There are new boutiques popping up by the day in Phnom Penh, and **Sihanouk Boulevard** is becoming quite the Oxford Street or Rodeo Drive of Cambodia – selling fashions at a fraction of the price of their western counterparts. Unlike Bangkok or Singapore, you won't find luxurious shopping malls with fashion stores in Cambodia, but there are pockets of upscale shops sprinkled throughout the city, as well as a couple of Japanese thrift shops offering clothes at ridiculously-low prices.

Medical Care

Since moving to Cambodia, we've had a number of occasions to experience the healthcare system. My husband has picked up many gastro-intestinal issues (very common in this part of the world) as well as dengue fever, so our visits to the clinic have been multiple. I've had neck pains and a touch of carpal tunnel syndrome, so have worked with a number of alternative practitioners in Phnom Penh.

Overall, we have been well taken care of. There are several clinics for expats and tourists in Cambodia where you'll find western doctors, as well as local practitioners who are caring and experienced in dealing with many of the basics. They are not always advisable for serious injuries or surgeries, however, and for those you'd need to take a trip to Bangkok or Singapore where you'll find world class care and medicine. Most places, including the hospital, expect cash or credit card payment at time of treatment.

In Phnom Penh, these are the recommended medical facilities:

SOS Clinic
International standard medical clinic with full facilities.
No. 161, Street 51 (corner of Street 242)
Tel: +855 (0)23-216911; +855 (0)12-816911
http://www.internationalsos.com/en/about-our-clinics_cambodia_35.htm

Naga Clinic
No. 11, Street 254 (between 51 and 55),
Tel: +855 (0)11-811175; +855 (0)23-211300
www.nagaclinic.com

Royal Rattanak Hospital
Full service international standard hospital affiliated with Bangkok Hospital, Thailand.
No.11, Street 592, Toul Kork
Tel: +855 (0)23-365555; +855 (0)99-631427; +855 (0)99-674303
www.royalrattanakhospital.com

Tropical & Travellers Medical Clinic
Clinic with British doctor.
No.88, Street 108
Tel: +855 (0)23-366802; +855 (0)12-898981
www.travellersmedicalclinic.com

Polyclinique Aurore
Local clinic, local doctors.
No. 58-60, Street 113 (off Sihanouk Blvd)

Tel: +855 (0)23-360152; +855 (0)12-779824; +855 (0)12-667561

Calmette Hospital
Main Hospital
No. 3, Monivong Blvd (near St. 80)
Tel: +855 (0)23-723 840

Sen Sok International University Hospital
No.91-96, Street 1986, Phnom Penh Thmey
Tel: +855 (0) 23 883 712

Royal Angkor International Hospital
Affiliated with Bangkok Hospital.
National Route #6 (Airport Road)
Tel: +855 (0)63 761 888, +855 (0)12 235 888, +855 (0)63 399 111
http://www.royalangkorhospital.com/en/default.asp

You'll also have a selection of choices and nationalities for alternative healthcare practitioners. I've visited a Korean acupuncturist, French physical therapist, English homeopath, and British trigger point massage therapist, all practicing in Phnom Penh. There's also a good selection of mental healthcare professionals and dentists (one of which is one of the world's largest private practices, with 52 dental chairs and internationally trained practitioners).

It's a good idea to check that your doctor has been trained overseas, as medical degrees in Cambodia are mostly inferior to those obtained in other countries.

Though the cost of doctor appointments is lower than in the west (SOS Clinic charges $68 - 85 for an appointment with a western doctor and $47 - 59 for a Cambodian doctor), it is always advisable to have medical insurance, particularly one which includes evacuation in case you need to be transported to Bangkok or Singapore (see *Travel Insurance*). A medical evacuation flight from Phnom Penh to Bangkok can cost $10,000-US$20,000 and will require payment up front. Serious medical problems without insurance can cost thousands of dollars at a good facility.

In order to take precautions and avoid medical facilities altogether, it's advisable to have a supply of hand sanitizer and to be vigilant about what you eat and drink. Peel your own fruit instead of buying it already peeled from the street, and make sure food is hot when you buy it from a local place or street vendor.

Pharmacies

There are a number of pharmacies around town but many of the smaller local ones sell inferior products, including counterfeit medications, so it's best to stick the main ones.

The most reputable pharmacies in Phnom Penh are:

Pharmacie De La Gare
Open: 7am – 7pm, Monday – Saturday and Sunday: 7pm – 5pm
No. 81Eo, Monivong Blvd (corner St. 108)
Tel: +855 (0)23-430205

U-Care Pharmacy (multiple locations): www.u-carepharmacy.com
Open: Monday – Sunday, 8am – 10pm
1) No 26 Sothearos Blvd, near St. 178
2) Sihanouk Boulevard, corner of St. 55
3) Norodom Blvd, corner of St. 136
4) No. 844, Kampuchea Krom, corner of St. 261
5) No. 254 Monivong Blvd, near St. 174
6) Sisowath Quay (riverside), near St. 136

Health Products Available

If you stick to the major pharmacies, you'll find almost everything you need, as well as medications from home that don't require you to have a prescription. Just take in the container and ask for a refill.

There isn't much you can't find, other than a few specific brand names, such as certain makes of contact lens solution or a particular moisturizer or shower gel. But, with all the development going on in Cambodia, that is changing by the day.

What's In Your Closet?

My closet contains hardly anything heavier than a long-sleeved top (for those air-conditioned spots or an occasional evening when the temperature falls below 75 degrees).

We were originally told by our volunteer organisation that we should dress conservatively – closed-toed shoes, no short skirts or revealing tops, and never to wear shorts in the office. But after living here for a few months, we discovered that it's fine to wear sandals and even nice flip-flops to work, and that clothing isn't as conservative for westerners as it is for Cambodians.

If you're working in a corporate environment, you may want to dress smartly, but attire is mostly casual wherever you go.

Several years ago, Cambodia was extremely conservative and westerners were frowned on for wearing revealing tops or skirts. Nowadays, however, it's quite permissible for a woman to wear a tank top or shorts as long as it's not too risqué. Men can wear sandals to work and open-necked shirts in most environments.

In small villages, however, you may want to cover up a bit more, since Cambodian villagers often don't have much exposure to westerners. You'll be stared at, no matter what you wear, so it is advisable to be a little more conservative and leave the tank top behind (or cover it with a short-sleeved top).

At the seaside or around a pool, you'll never see a Cambodian woman in a bathing suit. Locals swim fully dressed, as it's considered improper to show flesh in public. As a western woman, you're quite accepted in your bikini – just don't wear it inside.

Also remember that Cambodian weather is extreme, so you'll want to use protection against the sun in hot months (locals cover up in long sleeves, long trousers, hats, and gloves) as well as prepare yourself for the deluge in rainy season. It's too hot to wear a jacket or coat so you'll need a good umbrella, shoes you don't care much about, and one of those tiny, cheap (about 25 cents) raincoats which look like pink, blue, or yellow plastic bags with hoods and can be bought on street corners and most convenience stores.

There are opportunities in Phnom Penh and Siem Reap to dress up if you choose to, since there are many western hotels and restaurants and events, but casual is mostly fine.

When it comes to weddings, the same rule applies – for men. Fellows can show up in nice slacks and a shirt, but Cambodian women dress to the nines, taking many hours and numerous trips to the hair salon to be powdered, pampered, and adorned in floor-length sequined gowns for the occasion. As a western woman, you'll never be able (or desire) to compete, but you'll want to dress up a little bit to show you've made the effort. This may be the only opportunity you get to trot out the heels and don a glittery top, and I've even known western women to have an outfit made for the occasion.

On the subject of getting things made, Cambodia offers tailors by the dozen and you will find seamstresses anywhere (from local markets to main streets to back alleys) who can put together an outfit from scratch. Prices are low (I had a dress made for $17 plus the cost of fabric, which was $9) and expertise varies enormously, so ask around for a good tailor. You can take an item of clothing or show a picture in a book to have the design copied.

You can also get custom-made shoes at Beautiful Shoes on Street 143. Take in your own pair (or a picture), choose from dozens of different coloured leather swatches and you'll have a new pair within a week. The cost made ranges between $13 and $30, depending on what you order.

Holidays

Since Cambodia is a predominantly Buddhist country, many of the holidays are Buddhist celebrations based on lunar calendars, so the dates change from year to year.

It does, however, celebrate three new years: the International New Year on January 1, Chinese New Year later in January or early February, and Khmer New Year in April. Many of the holiday dates remain the same (or close to the same) and below are those for 2013 (those with an asterisk are changeable dates).

Holidays for 2013:

New Year's Day – 1 Jan
Victory over Genocide Day – 7 Jan
*Chinese New Year – 23 Jan

*Meak Bochea Day (A day for the veneration of Buddha and his teachings) – 27 Feb
International Women's Day – 8 March
*Khmer New Year – 13-16 April
International Labour Day – 1 May
*Royal Ploughing Ceremony (The start of ploughing season) – 28 May
King Sihamoni's Birthday – 13 May
*Visakha Bochea Day (Buddhist observance commemorating the birth, enlightenment, and passing of the Buddha) – 24 May
King's Mother's Birthday – 18 June
Constitution Day – 24 Sept
*Pchum Ben (Festival of the Ancestors) – 3-5 Oct
Norodom Sihanouk Commemoration Day - 15 Oct
King Sihamoni Coronation Day – 29 Oct
Independence Day – 9 Nov
*Water Festival (The end of the monsoon season with boat races and celebrations throughout the country.) – 16-18 Nov
International Human Rights Day – 10 Dec

Being Away From Family

Cambodia is a long way from most places, and it's a great distance to travel. Happily, Skype works well most of the time, and there are several airlines serving the region as well as AirAsia, which is an excellent low-cost airline (voted the world's best low cost carrier three years in a row by World Airline Awards). Sign up online at AirAsia.com to find out about specials being offered at various times during the year. I've bought tickets to Bangkok and Kuala Lumpur (the only places AirAsia flies to directly from Phnom Penh) for little more than a dollar (plus fees and surcharges), as well as a flight from Bangkok to Yangon, Myanmar for $3, and a flight from Kuala Lumpur to Kota Bharu in Malaysia for $20.

Living There With Kids

Life in Cambodia can provide an enriching, multi-cultural experience for any child. Western kids are doted upon by Cambodians and usually the subject of much photo-taking, cuddling, and cosseting from the time they are born. There may not be the same conveniences and distractions that you'll find in the west, but there's something healthier about having a smaller supply of TV programmes, computers, and other indoor attractions. While those distractions do exist here, kids in Cambodia spend more time outdoors, as well as playing with friends or taking part in after-school activities.

Some of the best-loved attractions for kids in Phnom Penh include the following:

- Kids' City - Opened June, 2013 on Sihanouk Blvd. Enormous entertainment complex for kids (and parents) featuring a climbing wall, ice rink, science centre, laser tag, playground, and coffee shops.
- Lyla Center (Street 508, near the Monivong Bridge). Indoor playground and lagoon in Phnom Penh with tubes, bridges and swimming areas for kids of all ages. There's also a dance studio, music school, gym, and cafe.
- Dragon Water Park in Dreamland (across from Naga World casino). Three pools, a slide, and a snack bar.
- Cambodian Equestrian Centre - Horse and pony lessons, board, competition, camp, party and show. Tel. 012 231 755; horsecambo@yahoo.com
- Bowling alley and bumper cars at Parkway Mall.
- Cartoons at the French Cultural Center every Saturday at 10 AM and children's library.
- Dreamland – Cambodia's first modern amusement park with funfair rides, dinosaur garden, bumper cars and food outlets. Sisowath Quay opposite Nagaworld.
- Group Magic Circus Solo - Theatre and circus performance artists. No.27BE, Street402 - +855 (0)12- 855072.
- Phnom Penh Water Park - Water park with water slides, wave pool and more - $3 weekends, $2 weekdays No.50, St.110 (Pochentong Rd) on the way to the airport. +855 (0) 23-881008.
- Peace Book Center and International Book Center are both good places for kid's art supplies, puzzles, and books. PBC is

153

on Monivong near St. 432, Street 271 and Sisowath Quay, and IBC has locations on Mao Tse Tung (next to Parkway centre), Kampuchea Krom Blvd near St. 215, Monivong Blvd near St. 174 and Sihanouk Blvd near St. 63.

- Sovanna Phum Arts Association - Shadow puppets, dance, music, and circus. Performances every Friday and Saturday at 7:30pm. No. 111, Street 360 (corner of Street 105). Tel: +855 (0)23- 987564.
- Phnom Tamao Wildlife Centre, Takeo province (about 45 minutes outside town by tuktuk). Tel: +855 (0) 12-842271.
- Riverside stroll – Boats of all shapes and sizes for viewing and riding.
- Royal Palace - Kids can play in a little traditional Khmer band where they can bang on drums and play the bells.
- Monkey Business – Large indoor playroom, with bouncy castles, slides, and a restaurant. 2nd Floor, Paragon Department Store, Street 214. Tel: +855 (0) 23-319319. The newest location is on Street 370 near Norodom Blvd and has a pool and climbing wall. Tel: +855 (0) 16 81 82 83.
- Lucky Kids' Club – Play area with books, toys and Saturday movies. Sihanouk Blvd above Lucky Burger.
- Happy City – Play area with trampoline, merry-go-round, and other games. Top floor of City Mall, Monireth Boulevard, next to Olympic Stadium.
- Kambol F1 Go Karts (for older kids) – Off Route 4 near the airport. (8km south of city centre). Formula 1 style go karts. Tel: +855 (0) 12-232332.

- Sorya Mall – Ice skating, roller skating, movies.
- Sovanna Shopping Centre – 4D adventure rides, games, movies.
- Quad biking (for older kids) – Outside town, near the Killing Fields. Tel: +855 (0)12-676381 or +855 (0) 12-676381

Pros & Cons

It takes a certain type of person to live in Cambodia.

While the country is beautiful and the people are wonderful, it's not a country to live in if you need a lot of creature comforts. You'll find excellent cuisine in elegant surroundings and be able to lounge next to swimming pools overlooking the Mekong if that's your desire, but that's not the real Cambodia.

Cambodia is still very much a third-world country - and it is evident everywhere. Sidewalks are broken up, corruption is blatant, and there's not a great deal of culture of the western variety. The weather is hot year-round, it's dusty and smelly in parts, and you'll see rats in the street. Newspapers are filled with stories about poor people being evicted from their land, girls being trafficked for sex, and garment factories exploiting their workers.

It's called the Wild Wild East for a reason.

The flip side is that you'll be exposed to a world where people are still gentle, respectful, and helpful – and somehow that makes everything all right in my world.

I love the "rough and ready" style of the place. The way traffic goes the wrong way on every street. And the feeling that I'm discovering something new every time I walk through town.

My husband and I realise (as do all our friends) that we will never understand what's going on here, no matter how long we live here. And once you get used to that concept, you can relax and enjoy it.

157

Living in Cambodia is much simpler than living in the west. We have no car. No bills (everything is paid in cash). No long commute to work.

Things happen more immediately. For example, when we first met our downstairs neighbour, he suggested getting together for a drink. Back home, that would have meant consulting spouses, checking calendars, and scheduling it for a week or two later. Here, we made a date for the same evening.

It's cheaper here. Meals out rarely cost more than $20 for two of us. We can get a bus to Kep or Siem Reap for less than $10 and stay in a decent hotel for $15 per night. The standard of living here means you get more for less.

The people are more playful, easy going, and accepting than anywhere we know. They may confuse you or misunderstand you, but they will never challenge or deliberately upset you.

Top Tips

There are two important things everyone needs to bring with them to Cambodia: patience and a sense of humour.

Know that you'll constantly be challenged and confused. And that sometimes your heart will break at the same time as it will sing.

Here are some tips I have for making the most of the experience:

Spend time with local people. Some of our best experiences have been visiting our tuktuk driver in his home or cooking dinner for him and his nine other relatives who unexpectedly showed up (Cambodians like to bring others along with them).

Go to a Cambodian wedding. Khmers love to include westerners in their celebrations, and weddings are sights to behold. If you work with Cambodians, it's pretty much guaranteed you'll be invited to one, even if you hardly know the bride or groom.

Respond to tuktuk and moto drivers. One of my pet peeves is seeing westerners ignoring tuktuk and moto drivers when they ask for a fare. They are rarely aggressive and will almost always reply with a smile and a nod when you say "*Ot tay akoon*" (no thank you).

Hire a regular tuktuk driver. It's a good idea to work with one or two drivers as you'll get to know them and their lives and, in turn, they will know your schedule so they are more available when you need them. It will also provide a driver with a regular wage.

Get out of the cities. The rural villages, back roads, and cultural centres show a more authentic side of Cambodia and you'll interact much more with locals when you leave town.

Learn the language. Even if you can only say a few phrases, give directions, and order in a restaurant, it's vitally important to know some Khmer if you're planning on making Cambodia your home (whether for six months or six decades).

Rent a motorbike. With a bike, you can explore the back roads and discover parts of the country you'd never see on a bus, car, or tuktuk. Always wear a helmet.

Slow down. Engage. Go for a walk in your neighbourhood. Talk to people along the way. Have a conversation with a tuktuk driver instead of brushing him off.

Be an ambassador for your country. Cambodian people tend to observe a lot and want to learn from foreigners. Remember that your actions are representative of your country, since Cambodians rarely travel overseas and may be looking at you to see how you operate.

Resources

Phnom Penh Guide for News, Festivals, Announcements, Information - phnompenh.gov.kh

LadyPenh (events around town) – ladypenh.com

Leng Pleng music guide – LengPleng.com

Cambodia Women in Business - facebook.com/Cambodia.WIB

Expat website for Cambodia - cambodia.alloexpat.com

Internations Cambodia - internations.org/cambodia-expats

Phnom Penh Visitors Guide - canbypublications.com

U.S. Department of State's current information on travel in Cambodia - travel.state.gov/travel/cis_pa_tw/cis/cis_1080.html

Pocket guide to Cambodia – CambodiaPocketGuide.com

Expat Blog - expat-blog.com/en/destination/asia/cambodia/

Cambo Guide - amboguide.com

International Christian Fellowship - icfpp.org

What To Expect

It's easy to know what you can *expect* in Cambodia: Nothing. That's one of the things I love about it. Nothing is predictable, everything changes, and you'll never figure it all out, no matter how long you live here.

But there are a few things you *can* expect as there's a better than average chance the following things will happen:

- *Your bus will break down*
- *Your power will go out*
- *You'll get a stomach bug*
- *You'll get the wrong dish in a restaurant*

- *Your tuktuk driver will get lost*
- *You'll be awakened at 4am by chanting monks*
- *You'll be caught in a downpour*
- *You'll be a victim of petty theft*
- *You'll find yourself in a squat toilet with no paper*
- *Your meeting will be cancelled*
- *Your deadline will change*

But you'll also experience vivid sunsets over ancient temples, hear tiny voices of wide-eyed children calling out to you, bask in the gentle smile of a saffron-wrapped monk, and celebrate a race of people who give unconditionally, love warmly, and enrich your life in more ways than you thought possible.

This, my friends, is Cambodia.

Author

Gabrielle Yetter is a published writer who started her career as a journalist on *The Star* newspaper in South Africa. She has worked in the US and UK and is now living in Cambodia, where she volunteers for an NGO and works as a freelance writer. Her work has been published in Southeast Asia Globe, AsiaLife, Latitudes, Khmer440, Expat Advisory, and Mighty Mercury and she recently completed a book about traditional desserts in Cambodia ("The Sweet Tastes of Cambodia") which was published in December 2012. She has lived in India, Bahrain, England, and the U.S. and loves to explore the world and eat cupcakes (not necessarily in that order). Examples of her writing can be seen on GabrielleYetter.com.

Editors & Photographers

Dr. Jessie Voigts has a PhD in International Education, and is constantly looking for ways to increase intercultural understanding, especially with kids (it's never too young to start!). She has lived and worked in Japan and London, and traveled around the world. Jessie is the publisher of **Wandering Educators**, a travel library for people curious about the world. She founded the Family Travel Bloggers Association, and the Youth Travel Blogging Mentorship Program. She's published six books about travel and intercultural learning, with more on the way. You can usually find her family by water – anywhere in the world.

Brianna Krueger is an aspiring novelist and constant dreamer. She has a BA in English: Creative Writing, Sociology, and Gender and Women's Studies from Western Michigan University. Brianna is currently chief editor of Wandering Educators.

Emma Pot is a 22-year-old journalism student attending Windesheim University in Zwolle, The Netherlands. She has made videos for Dutch foundations and travelled throughout SE Asia taking photographs.

Mark Reibman is a commercial and travel photographer who relocated to Cambodia in 2012. Originally from Seattle, USA, he specializes in architectural and interior photography, hotel and restaurant photography, travel and cultural photography, and portrait photography.

Cover photo: **John Rizzo** is an award winning photojournalist and educator who leads worldwide photo tours for photographers of all levels and whose work has been published in *Newsweek, The New York Times, The Overseas Press Club, Bloomberg, The Los Angeles Times, The Washington Post, Fortune,* and *Money Magazine.*

All photos courtesy and copyright Gabrielle Yetter, Emma Pot, Mark Reibman, and John Rizzo.

Made in the USA
San Bernardino, CA
16 December 2014